PLACES *of* TRANQUILITY

PLACES *of* TRANQUILITY

(Originally titled PLACES OF INSPIRATION)

JAMES PIPKIN

Foreword by Anthony Storr

BALLANTINE BOOKS NEW YORK

To Jeanne

Text and photographs copyright © 1990 by James Pipkin

Foreword copyright © 1990 Anthony Storr

All rights reserved under International and Pan-American Copyright
Conventions. Published in the United States by Ballantine Books,
a division of Random House, Inc., New York, and distributed
in Canada by Random House of Canada Limited, Toronto.
Originally published in Great Britain as *Places of Inspiration* by
Pavilion Books Limited.

Library of Congress Cataloging-in-Publication Data

Pipkin, James. 1939-
    Places of tranquility/James Pipkin.
        p.   cm.
    Includes bibliographical references.
    ISBN 0-345-36261-6
    1. Sacred space—Pictorial works. I. Title.
BL580.P56   1990   89-49740
304.2—dc20   CIP

Manufactured in Italy

First American Edition: November 1990

10 9 8 7 6 5 4 3 2 1

CONTENTS

'When from our better selves we have too long
Been parted by the hurrying world, and droop,
Sick of its business, of its pleasures tired,
How gracious, how benign, is Solitude.'

William Wordsworth, *The Prelude* Book Fourth

FOREWORD

We live at a period of history when Western culture assumes that personal relationships are the key to happiness. If an individual wishes to seek solitude, it is often implied that there must be something wrong with him or her. This is a modern aberration, which is partly dependent on the decline of religious faith. When people believed that their relationship with God was more important than their relationship with spouse, lover, or children, it was understood that there might be times in their lives when it was necessary or desirable to leave family and friends for a while in order to pray in solitude, renew religious faith, or wait upon God for inspiration or healing.

Jesus set the example by spending forty days in the wilderness before returning to proclaim his message. St Catherine of Siena spent three years in seclusion before embarking upon her career of preaching and teaching. St Ignatius Loyola spent nearly a year as a beggar in Manresa, often spending seven or more hours in solitary prayer in a cave outside the town. Each year, Mahomet retreated to the cave of Hera for the month of Ramadan. Franz Liszt expressed the essence of such religious experiences in one of the most beautiful of his pieces for solo piano, *Bénédiction de Dieu dans la solitude*.

In contemporary Western society, many people find it hard to subscribe to any orthodox faith or to believe in a personal Deity. But this does not mean that these varieties of spiritual experience have lost their value, or that the need for them is any less pressing. Indeed, this need may be more urgent today than it was for past generations. Modern urban life tends to overload the sensorium. It is difficult to escape from the noise of traffic and aircraft, from radio and television, or from the intrusion of the telephone. More than ever before we need the peace of solitude and the opportunity to explore our inner depths. But contemporary assumptions have made it more difficult for those who feel a desire for self-renewal to find a reason for seeking it without being dubbed 'selfish' or 'neurotic'. We have not developed a secular language to describe the inner psychological experiences for which the mystics used religious terms. But the 'peace of God which passeth understanding' still exists, whether or not we believe in God or have the words for it.

Throughout history, many individuals have described moments of harmony, of utter peace and tranquility, of being at one with both oneself and the universe, which have come to them when alone and which have equalled or surpassed any ecstatic experience of being in love or feeling of union with another person.

Very frequently, experiences of this kind occur when the individual is alone in the countryside. They often date from childhood. Wordsworth records:

> There was a time when meadow, grove, and stream,
> The earth and every common sight,
> To me did seem
> Apparelled in celestial light,
> The glory and the freshness of a dream.[1]

Many other writers, including Walt Whitman, A. L. Rowse, Arthur Koestler, Bernard Berenson, and C. S. Lewis, have recorded mystical feelings of transcendent unity with nature or of being in touch with an ultimate order of reality which gave a new meaning to existence. These experiences usually come unsought. They just happen, for reasons which no-one can determine and they can happen almost anywhere. Koestler experienced feelings of this kind when held in solitary confinement in a Spanish prison. Scientists have described comparable ecstasies after the solution of a difficult problem.

More commonly, these experiences occur when the subject is in natural surroundings. Those who want to repeat the experience sometimes seek places on earth which are remote or difficult of access. An extreme example is that of the American explorer, Admiral Byrd, who, in 1934, manned an advanced weather base in the Antarctic entirely alone. On his daily walk, he paused to 'listen to the silence'.

Here were imponderable processes of the cosmos, harmonious and soundless. Harmony, that was it! That was what came out of the silence – a gentle rhythm, the strain of a perfect chord, the music of the spheres, perhaps. It was enough to catch that rhythm, momentarily to be myself a part of it. In that instant I could feel no doubt of man's oneness with the universe.[2]

This characteristic account illustrates the difficulty of describing the ineffable in words. Those who have never had such an experience may dismiss it as illusory; but those who have shared comparable feelings will recognize Byrd's account as authentic, even though they might try to express them in different words.

Fortunately, those in search of inner harmony and peace do not have to follow Admiral Byrd to the Antarctic to match his encounter with cosmic harmony. As this book demonstrates, place is an important determinant of inspiration; but the place selected need not be impossibly remote or difficult of access. James Pipkin has chosen examples of deserts, caves, mountains, seacoasts, and gardens. Most of these places seem to me to have one thing in common. Their beauties reach beyond the personal, making the individual who contemplates them feel that his own problems and concerns are trivial or mundane. At first sight, gardens, because they are man-made, might seem an exception. But gardens, like great works of art and architecture, can sometimes provide a resting-place of such tranquility that they too can induce a state of inner harmony.

James Pipkin tells us that the travels which made this book possible enabled him to make progress in his personal search for tranquility. Most of us will never be able to reach all the places which he visited; but his beautiful photographs are themselves an inspiration. Everyone who owns this book will turn to it again and again as a source of solace and refreshment.

Anthony Storr, Oxford 1990

1 William Wordsworth, *Intimations of Immortality from Recollections of Early Childhood.*
2 Richard E. Byrd, *Alone*, (London: Harborough, 1958), pp. 62–3.

INTRODUCTION

THE ROLE OF PLACES OF TRANQUILITY AND INSPIRATION

In AD 651, a shepherd boy named Cuthbert entered a monastery in Scotland. Cuthbert's wisdom and holiness attracted many followers. He became a teacher and an administrator, and he was named Bishop of Lindisfarne. Yet Cuthbert (later St Cuthbert) felt the greatest happiness as a hermit, alone in a simple stone cell on a small island off the northeast coast of England, and that is where he went to live until his death.[1] Surrounded by the 'deep and infinite sea', his solitude was the reward for a lifetime of community service, and Cuthbert 'rejoiced that . . . he had earned his right to climb to the quiet of meditation upon God'.[2]

In the seventeenth century, a man who had been an attendant to Japan's Shogun sought tranquility in a garden he had designed specifically for contemplation. Sitting in meditation on a deck of his house, he could look out at a white sand garden, the flowering bushes that bordered it, a small waterfall, an ancient sazanqua tree, and a green hillside with maple trees and mosses. In this setting he was able to find peace.

In the middle of the nineteenth century, Sir Richard Burton was irresistibly drawn to the desert. He described 'the drear silence, the solitude, and the fantastic desolation' of the desert. 'Though your mouth glows, and your skin is parched . . . your sight brightens . . . and your spirits become exuberant; your fancy and your imagination are powerfully aroused, and the wildness and sublimity of the scenes around you stir up all the energies of your soul . . . .' After experiencing the tranquility of the desert, he found 'real pain in returning to the turmoil of civilization'.[3]

In the 1890s, a Swiss teenager named Carl Gustav Jung was lonely and troubled. He could not help asking difficult questions, especially about religion, and his parents and teachers often responded with anger and condemnation. One day

MATIRA BEACH, BORA BORA, FRENCH POLYNESIA.

Jung's father gave him a ticket to go on a cog railway to the top of a mountain called the Rigi. The mountain was taller than anything Jung had ever seen, and, as he ascended, Jung was 'speechless with joy'. He stood on the top, breathing the 'strange thin air' and 'looking into unimaginable distances'. He thought to himself that at last he was seeing 'the real world', where there are 'no unanswerable questions, where one can *be* without having to ask anything'. He was silent, recognizing that he was in God's domain. Many years later, in his old age, Jung recalled that the experience was 'the best and most precious gift' his father ever gave him.[4]

These four situations involve a variety of motivations, objectives and circumstances. Yet they all represent a universal phenomenon: at some points in our lives, all of us experience a need to go off by ourselves, away from the pressures and anxieties of communal life, and to find a place of solitude. That need is timeless, and throughout history certain places have exerted a particular attraction when people have felt the need to be alone.

This is a book about those special places, places of tranquility and inspiration. For me they are the most wonderful locations on this planet, and I offer this book as a celebration of them, a celebration of both the external qualities of the sites and the internal stirrings they generate.

The places, and the reasons we seek them, are varied. The purpose may be as simple as getting away from day-to-day pressures and rejuvenating the mind and body. It may involve contemplation of our purpose in life. It may be religious – a quest for divine inspiration. Whatever the reason, there is a common objective, which has to do with quieting the mind and achieving inner peace. In the silence, we open ourselves to deep understanding and to flashes of insight that may even rise to the level of inspiration.

That quest has been given many names. In Zen terms, attaining an inner tranquility is experiencing the 'still center of eternity' or 'enlightenment'. Others describe it as Nirvana, Tao, Atman, or as finding heaven on earth.

Many of the places to which that quest leads involve nature, and I have selected four categories of places that have exerted a special appeal over the centuries. Those categories are deserts, caves, mountains, and seacoasts. I have also included a pilgrimage site (the Ganges at Varanasi) and several examples of

SUNRISE AT WHITE HOUSE OVERLOOK, CANYON DE CHELLY, ARIZONA.

gardens designed as places, at least in part, of contemplation or spiritual nourishment: Japanese Zen gardens, Islamic gardens, and British woodland gardens (together with their predecessor, the sacred grove). Some of the sites selected have been visited by man since prehistoric times, and many were regarded as sacred by earlier people.

It would be misleading to suggest that the places described in this book are potential panaceas for all of our problems. A quiet place does not ensure a quiet mind, and there are many examples of unsuccessful searches for inner peace. In the end, peace is a function of the mind and not of geography.

However, such places played an important part in man's search for inner peace in centuries past and continue to do so today. They provide an environment that facilitates the process of quieting the mind. They make day-to-day problems seem distant and inconsequential. Most significantly, they help bring to the consciousness basic values that have been forgotten or suppressed – values having to do with the nature of true contentment and the relative unimportance of much that we pursue.

THE ATLANTIC FROM ACADIA NATIONAL PARK, MAINE.

OUR CLOUDED VISION

One of the underlying premises of this book can best be explained by reference to the photograph of Mount Batur in Bali (page 103). When you go off by yourself to seek peace and understanding, the physical destination may be a monastery, a mountaintop, a seaside retreat, or a private oasis. Whatever the destination, by acknowledging the quest, you are implicitly recognizing that your vision is clouded and that you cannot see clearly in the direction of something that you really want to see.

Suddenly, often at an unexpected time, the clouds part and something appears. The vision is not entirely clear; there is some mystery about it. The vision represents a clue, a stimulus to further exploration, something to lead you on, something that represents a connection in the mind, something that reinforces and recognizes a fact you knew on a deep level but could not bring to the surface. You see reality in a different way; a piece of the puzzle somehow falls into place.

That is what happened with Mount Batur. I was in Bali to experience and photograph the sacred mountains. I arose long before dawn and drove for several hours along narrow, twisting, pot-holed roads to be near Mount Batur at sunrise. The dawn came and I was surrounded by dense fog. I could see only a few feet, and I was frustrated. Half an hour later, I could see some trees a hundred yards away. After another hour, with no warning, the fog and clouds parted to afford a brief glimpse of the summit of Mount Batur and then closed again.

That fleeting view – the colors, the drifting clouds, the ethereal quality, the sense of looking through a shifting, irregular frame – was astonishing. In contrast, an hour later Mount Batur was revealed with total clarity. There were no clouds; every form was sharp, every detail was disclosed, and the effect was completely different. The earlier mysterious, momentary appearance was magical; the subsequent total revelation was mundane and uninspiring.

What does that tell us? We think that we want to see the objective clearly, that we want to know where we will be in our lives many years in the future. We think we want someone to tell us what we should do next. However, that approach does not work. We learn what gives us feelings of fulfillment and contentment primarily through those momentary synapses, those rare occasions of insight and inspiration that provide clues (rather than definitive answers) with respect to our personal vision.

Though frustrating, that result is for the best. If we knew what the future looked like with precision, the stimulus would be quite different. Sometimes, when we are engaged in an arduous task, we look back and say that we never would have started if we had known what it was going to be like. Yet with our clouded vision and momentary insights, we are encouraged to take another step and see what lies ahead. We start up a twisting mountain path, intending to go only far enough to see what is around the next bend. The human spirit being what it is, we may wind up going to the top of the mountain. In the end, we usually find we have accomplished something that is worthwhile.

So it is for me with the photograph of Mount Batur. Although not among the most beautiful images in this book, it evokes for me a special feeling, a spirituality, that is indicative of what personal quests (and this book) are all about. It speaks of peace and movement at the same time. It is tranquil yet not static. It urges us onward.

KEYS TO THE EXPERIENCE

Writing a book often has as much to do with educating the author as with the author's desire to communicate. The process of researching this book was part of my own inner search. I tried to visit locations in a way that would be meaningful for me, while also obtaining the information and photographs that would be used in the book. That was not always easy.

I tend to run around, 'accomplishing' as much as possible, squeezing many things into a short period of time. In some ways, this is satisfying; in others, it is frustrating. There never is enough time, and often, by concentrating exclusively on the end result, I forget to enjoy the process of getting there. Once the result is achieved, there is always something else to take its place – another dragon to slay. The time for enjoyment never arrives.

In planning trips for this book, I resolved to make some changes. Sometimes I succeeded; sometimes I fell back into old patterns. I had some of the most wonderful experiences in my life, as may come through, for example, in my description of Milford Sound. Others were disappointments, although that was often a product of my own overly ambitious scheduling. Fortunately, I learned as I went along.

The most important lesson was to allow more time than I thought I would need – time not only for logistical obstacles and delays caused by the weather, but time to return to each location on several occasions. On the first visit, I gathered information, made a general reconnaissance, and took basic photographs. Subsequent visits provided the opportunity to see the place at different times of day, to focus on elements of special appeal, to observe in an unhurried fashion, and generally to intensify the experience – to let the place sink in on a deep level. More often than not, it was the subsequent visits that provided the insights, the different way of looking at a familiar subject, and the vivid memories.

It was also important for me to go at times when crowds were absent and distractions minimized. Usually, this meant as early and as late as feasible. A number of solitary experiences at dawn were especially rewarding.

Another key was opening myself to the timelessness of the place. I tried to imagine myself in an earlier time and to feel how the original inhabitants would have experienced the site. If that required meditation, or physically making contact with the natural elements of the site, I tried to give myself freedom to do it. I often observed others doing the same.

A particularly striking example occurred on my visit to the megaliths at Carnac, in France. Here, long rows of huge stones cover parts of the landscape. The significance of the stones is not known with certainty; about all we know is that the formations date back thousands of years before the Christian era and that the stones went beyond pure function and extended to something symbolic and spiritual.

One of the largest stones (the giant of Manio) stands alone in a clearing in a wooded area. One day I sat and watched for several hours as a succession of visitors approached the stone. Most of them placed their hands on the stone and stood in silence with their eyes closed. Many also touched the stone with their foreheads or bodies. One could easily dismiss such behavior as foolish, but for me it was a moving experience. The people (mainly from West Germany) were opening themselves to the possibility that a particular energy was associated with that place and that stone. They wanted to feel that energy. These were people in their forties, fifties, and sixties from a highly civilized, urbanized society. They were responding to an instinctive need to connect with nature and ancient wisdom, a need that seems to be experienced by people all over the earth.

In general, the places described in this book are not only beautiful but also spiritual. Many were considered sacred by their early inhabitants. In visiting and learning about these places, I was struck by how many times a new group had come along and imposed its will on the original inhabitants, often in the name of religion. The conquerors had found the 'true religion' and sought to enlighten the heathen, by force if necessary. They tried to control the beliefs of their new subjects, and they changed the form of the place. A sacred spring or sacred burial ground was covered by a church; a Hindu shrine was destroyed and replaced by a mosque; missionaries in the Americas or Polynesia prohibited local religious practices and substituted their own; ancient cliff dwellings occupied by Huguenots were destroyed by Catholics; sanctuaries of nature-worshipping people were characterized as the work of the devil and torn down.

Gradually, we are beginning to realize how much was lost. We are recognizing the senselessness of these actions and how misguided it is for one group to consider itself 'good' or 'right' and another group with different ideas 'evil' or

'wrong'. In addition, all around the world, there is a growing awareness of the possibility that the ancient people had something to say – people who regarded ceremony and sacred rite as a part of everyday life and who recognized the divine in every animal, plant, tree, or rock.

To some, this may seem rather a romantic notion. The fact that earlier people took only what they needed from nature can be viewed as a rational decision, essential to their survival, rather than a product of their spirituality. Whatever the motivation, however, it seems indisputable that the ancient people lived more in harmony with nature than does urban twentieth-century man.

Most individuals in today's urban societies have little contact with nature. In early times, a man killed an animal because his family was hungry. In this age of specialization, one group kills an animal, another transports it, another sells it wholesale, and another sells it retail. Each group views its activities as a matter of economics. The ultimate consumer takes no responsibility for the killing of the animal or the consequences of that action.

Yet the potentially disastrous changes now taking place in our environment are forcing us to realize that we cannot continue to compartmentalize our vision and justify our actions on the basis of personal (or national) short-term economics. We are beginning to accept that our longer-term survival requires each of us to take a broad view – a view that becomes meaningful only when we experience some personal reconnection with nature.

I believe that the need to reconnect is in part responsible for the increased interest in the kinds of places pictured in this book. However little we may understand it, there is something therapeutic that draws us to the unspoiled places in nature and something that causes us to feel that the people who came to those places in earlier, simpler times possessed knowledge that is important to our own well-being.

THE SELECTION PROCESS

This book is neither a comprehensive listing of all the inspirational settings in the world nor a selection of the 'top 25'. Most of us have our own special place or places where we have our most peaceful moments. Often such a place relates to a childhood experience or to where a person was when some particularly happy event occurred. For some it may be a simple room set aside for privacy and

MONT ST MICHEL, FRANCE.

solitude. For others, unplanned combinations of mood and setting have led to inspirational experiences. No single volume could do justice to all such places.

My approach was to concentrate on representative examples, all of which some way relate to nature in some manner. I omitted most man-made places of retreat, except for certain structures that are located where they are *because* of the natural setting – for example, the temples on Bali's sacred mountains and the Turkish monastery carved out of volcanic ash. With the exception of gardens, locations were included only if there is something about the site itself, apart from what man placed there, that traditionally has drawn people to it.

Sometimes the current popularity of the place was a factor in deciding whether it should be included. Although a location may have been regarded as a place of tranquility or inspiration for hundreds of years, if it is currently so overrun with visitors that quiet contemplation is not possible, it was omitted. In this respect, the Taj Mahal was a close call. For much of the day, the Taj Mahal is anything but peaceful; however, in the half-hour just before and after sunrise, the Taj is serene and has a presence that causes visitors to watch in respectful silence. On that basis, and because the Taj Mahal is an example of Islamic garden design, I included it.

Similarly, although Ulu Watu, the picturesque temple on the coast of Bali, is a popular place around sunset, by moving a few yards away, I was able to enjoy the magnificence of the setting unaware of the proximity of others. In other words, popularity alone did not disqualify a subject; it could be included as long as the visitor who desires solitude may still find a quiet spot and enjoy the qualities that have always brought people to the place.

Remoteness was not in itself a qualification. While I recognize the appeal of relatively inaccessible places, I did not want to limit this book to places that have only been seen by a few people or that can be reached only by the most agile and best conditioned individuals. I preferred that the selections be reasonably accessible to anyone who makes the effort to go and that the examples selected be suggestive rather than definitive. If you resonate to one of the categories covered in the book but want to go somewhere more remote than the places pictured here, so much the better.

Two other examples may help to explain my thought process. The site of Mont St Michel, in Normandy on the coast of France, has been a magnet for

MATIRA BEACH, BORA BORA.

thousands of years. The rocky mound, formerly called Mont Tombe, is believed to have been a site of Druidic worship and in Celtic times was thought of as a refuge of dead souls. Legend has it that the first Christian church was erected after the Archangel Michael appeared in a dream to the Bishop of Avranches and commanded him to build a sanctuary there. By the early medieval period, the site was a place of pilgrimage.

The problem is that Mont St Michel today is overwhelmed with tourists. Anywhere close to the abbey, you feel that you are in a sea of people, bounded by souvenir shops and cafes. Peaceful contemplation is possible only at a distance.

French Polynesia posed another problem. The first Europeans to arrive there were explorers – Samuel Wallis and Louis Antoine de Bougainville in 1767 and Captain Cook two years later. They were enchanted by what they saw, natives living apparently happily and without guile. The land was beautiful, flowers were everywhere, and fruit trees, fish, and water were abundant. Sex was openly enjoyed and made available freely to the Europeans. The explorers returned home with superlatives about the tropical paradise they had found. Bougainville wrote:

'I felt as though I had been transported to the Garden of Eden. Everywhere we found hospitality, peace, innocent joy and every appearance of happiness. What a country! What a people!'[5]

Captain Cook's naturalist described Tahiti as 'the truest picture of an Arcadia', adding ominously, 'of which we were going to be kings'.[6] Soon, other Europeans arrived, with sicknesses unknown to Polynesia, with greed, with an intent to exploit, and with a determination to impose their religious beliefs on the natives. Within a short time, the spirit of the natives was broken, paradise was destroyed, and the population went into decline. In the nineteenth century, when artists and writers like Gauguin and Melville arrived, they found a Tahiti that bore little resemblance to the place described by early explorers.

Today, French Polynesia retains a rare physical beauty, and it continues to be regarded as an idyllic vacation spot. It can be tranquil and relaxing. Yet because of its history, and because of the apparent sadness of its people, I decided not to feature it.

With that introduction to the selection process, we turn to some of the locations that, for various reasons, I consider 'places of tranquility and inspiration'.

SUNSET AT POFAI BAY, BORA BORA.

Part One

DESERTS

PLACES OF PURIFICATION

THE PYRAMIDS OF GIZA, EGYPT.

Deserts are harsh and inhospitable to man. The heat is intense; water and food supplies are limited; mere survival is difficult. Yet for those who choose the path of self-denial and asceticism, deserts have always been attractive.

Many biblical figures received inspiration in the desert. Moses lived quietly in the desert for forty years, and many early Christian recluses withdrew to the desert. In the fourth century, thousands followed the example of the 'Desert Fathers' (including St Paul, St Anthony, and St Jerome), who chose the desert's austerity, hardships, and solitude as a means of pursuing their religious objectives. Since the desert landscape is one of emptiness, it is viewed as a place to find divine revelation.

That approach was not limited to Christianity. In a number of countries, holy men (and others) have deliberately experienced the unrelenting heat, the simplicity of lifestyle, and the absence of distractions that the deserts represent. Through fiery heat comes purification and transformation. 'The desert is the domain of the sun, of the pure and blinding light which is the realization of truth.'[1]

Three examples of settings in desert or semi-desert regions are described here. Ayers Rock has been a special place for Australian aboriginals for at least thirty thousand years, and the natives who remain in that area consider it their duty to look after their sacred sites and to hand on the songs, stories, and ceremonies that relate to those sites.

The Sahara is the archetypal desert – vast, arid, largely devoid of vegetation, and blazingly hot. The deserts of Egypt were the places where kings were buried; later, the solitude of the deserts attracted literally thousands of early Christian hermits.

Monument Valley, in Utah and Arizona, was formerly a home of the Anasazi and today is part of the Navajo reservation. It is an inhospitable place in which to live; the soil is poor, water is limited, and temperatures can be extreme. Yet the Navajos believe it is part of the land where they are supposed to be, and so they stay, despite the hardships.

AYERS ROCK

Australia

Ayers Rock, often said to be the largest monolith in the world, thrusts upward to a height of eleven hundred feet from the flat desert floor of central Australia. The visible part is like the tip of an iceberg; the rock extends downward for several miles. Sometimes described as sandstone, it is more accurately termed a sedimentary conglomerate, consisting of rounded pebbles or boulders cemented together in layers.

The scientific theory as to how the rock was created has to do with weathering and erosion over the ages. There is another theory, thousands of years older, that forms part of the mythology of the people who have inhabited the area for at least the last thirty thousand years[2] – the Aboriginals (or Anangu) of central Australia. That theory has to do with the 'Dreamtime' (Tjukurpa).

Prior to the Dreamtime, it is said, the world was featureless. During Tjukurpa, giant mythical beings traversed the surface, wandering from place to place and creating the natural features that we now see. When the Dreamtime came to an end, the great creatures died, and natural features mark the places of their death.

Several stories concern Ayers Rock, or Uluru as it is known to the Aboriginals. According to the Aboriginals, two boys who were playing in the mud

ABOVE: ABORIGINAL PAINTINGS IN A CAVE AT THE BASE OF THE ROCK.
LEFT: EARLY MORNING AT AYERS ROCK.

after a rain created the muddy mound that became Uluru. Later, animals passing through the area gave additional form to the rock. For example, two blue-tongued lizards killed an emu and cut up its meat with a stone axe. Large joints of the emu's meat survive as slabs of rock. When two bell-bird brothers arrived and asked to share the emu, the lizards greedily retained most of the meat for themselves. The bell-birds set fire to the lizard men's shelter. Lichen on the rock face is the smoke from the fire, and the lizard men, who burned to death, became two half-burned boulders.[3]

The Aboriginals believe that the characters in these stories are their direct ancestors. Soon after birth, each individual is identified with a specific ancestral being. Individuals perform the same rituals and follow the same life as their ancestors did during the Dreamtime. Their ancestors were, in their belief, both actual persons and totemic beings. What they did during the Dreamtime 'must now be done in ritual, and the places associated with them must be visited and cared for'.[4] Through such deeds lies the 'promise of . . . the after-life, where game abound[s], [where] there [is] soft grass to lie on, refreshing streams, and soft breezes'.[5] During life, an individual recreates his ancestral world; 'on death a person becomes his dreaming'.[6]

The activities of the Aboriginal ancestors have also been described in terms of the 'dreaming-tracks', or 'songlines', that they made and the effect that those tracks have on present-day Aboriginals. As Bruce Chatwin wrote:

'. . . each totemic ancestor, while traveling through the country, was thought to have scattered a trail of words and musical notes along the line of his footprints . . . .'

'A song . . . was both map and direction-finder. Providing you knew the song, you could always find your way across country.'[7]

For present-day Aboriginals, the aim of their religious life is 'to keep the land the way it was and should be'. As a result: 'The man who [goes] "Walkabout" [is] making a ritual journey. He [treads] in the footprints of his Ancestor. He [sings] the Ancestor's stanzas without changing a word or note – and so recreate[s] the Creation.'[8]

Uluru, or Ayers Rock, is a point where the tracks of several ancestral groups crossed. Uluru, like Atila (Mount Conner) and Katatjuta (the Olgas), is a crossroads – a refuge and base camp – of the Aboriginal people of central

SUNRISE AT AYERS ROCK.

DAWN AT AYERS ROCK.

Australia.[9] Each group 'is obliged to look after the dreaming places, or sacred sites, created by the ancestral heroes in its estate, and to hand on the traditional songs, stories and ceremonies that commemorate the ancestors' adventures in that territory.'[10]

Aboriginal people in the Pitjantjatjara and Yankunyjatjara tribes remain in the area today, keeping contact with their ancestors' spirits by maintaining their songs and legends, performing their rituals, and keeping the land as unchanged as possible. In recent years, hotels and commercial facilities have been relocated away from the rock. Certain sacred areas have been fenced to prevent intrusion. In 1985, title to the land was handed back to the traditional owners, subject to a 99-year lease to the Australian National Parks and Wildlife Service. Uluru National Park is now administered by a trust whose governing body includes Aboriginal representatives.

At present, the park is visited by almost 250,000 people each year. For the majority, a visit consists mainly of a sunset view of the rock and, for those who are physically fit, a climb to its summit. A visit may also include a quick coach trip to the Olgas or a half-hour helicopter tour.

Sunset is observed from a special viewing area to the west of the rock. There are often as many as thirty coaches in that area as well as a large number of automobiles. People line up, virtually shoulder to shoulder, to watch the rock change colors. As soon as the last ray of sunlight is off the rock, they pile back into their coaches and head for the hotels. Within fifteen minutes after sunset, the viewing area is deserted.

The magic, however, continues. The sky around the Olgas, where the sun has set, glows bright orange. That glow continues to illuminate Ayers Rock, which takes on a subtle, gentle quality. In the sky on both sides of the rock, a blue band appears above the horizon, with a pink band above it. Scanning upward, the pink gradually changes to ivory and back to blue, a blue that becomes richer and darker as the eye ascends. Stars begin to assert their presence. The park is virtually silent, and its majesty and tranquility are clearly felt.

Even more peaceful is the hour immediately before dawn. The horizon becomes outlined by a faint glow in the sky, silhouettes of trees and rocks begin to appear, and the light show of the previous night is repeated in reverse as the desert comes back to life.

ABOVE: EVENING TWILIGHT AT AYERS ROCK.
RIGHT: LIKE AYERS ROCK, THE OLGAS RISE ABRUPTLY FROM
THE DESERT PLAIN IN CENTRAL AUSTRALIA.

THE DESERTS OF EGYPT

The Egyptian deserts west of the Nile are part of the Sahara, the hottest and driest desert in the world. The Sahara is often thought of as vast expanses of sand, but it is also plateaus of limestone and sandstone, ancient riverbeds, and valleys hollowed out by wind and water over the millenia. It is a place where god-kings were buried in expectation of eternal life. It is a place where priests developed centers of study and where they acquired sophisticated practical knowledge of mathematics, astronomy, surveying, chemistry, and metallurgy.

For almost two thousand years, the deserts of Egypt have attracted people who chose to reject the world and pursue a contemplative life. Many of these have been Christians, including St Paul, the first of the Desert Fathers. Paul was born in Alexandria in AD 228. When he was a young man, the Christians were persecuted, and Paul left the city and went to live in the desert. He lived alone in a cave, which he sometimes shared with wild animals. It is said that he was fed by crows, and that he spent his life in prayer and contemplation; he was also a healer and protector of Bedouins who roamed the area.[11]

In about AD 270, the man who was later called St Anthony heard the gospel being read and felt it was being spoken directly to him: 'Go sell all that thou hast, and give it to the poor, and thou shalt have treasure in heaven, and come and follow me. . . .' St Anthony sold his possessions and became a hermit in the desert. Others followed him into the wilderness, emulating his asceticism, and in time a large community of hermits developed around St Anthony's cell. His experience became the prototype for Christian monasticism, a way of life leading to salvation.[12]

In the fourth and fifth centuries, Christians flocked to the deserts of Egypt. At one time there were seven thousand men and women living in various congregations near Tabenna, five thousand monks on Mount Nitria, and ten thousand monks at Arsinoe. One traveler reported the 'dwellers in the desert as all but equal to the population of the towns'.

SUNSET NEAR THE MONASTERY OF ST CATHERINE, THE SINAI, EGYPT.

To some, it seemed that the monks were trying to outdo each other in kindness and goodness or in how little food they consumed (one monk was said to have lived on five dry figs a day and another was said to have lived for thirty years on nothing but barley bread and muddy water). As the popularity of monasticism increased, so did the doubts of some of the skeptics. Though most observers continued to recognize the noble purpose of the monks and their quest for truth through purification, others described the 'ascetic epidemic' in less laudatory terms. Lecky complained that a 'hideous, distorted and emaciated maniac, without knowledge, without patriotism, without natural affection, spending his life in a long routine of useless and atrocious self-torture, and quailing before the ghastly phantoms of his delirious brain, had become the ideal . . . .'[13]

Eventually, the popularity of asceticism in the deserts of Egypt waned; however, many of the monasteries that were established during this period remain occupied today, and in the twentieth century there has been a resurgence of interest in the lifestyle represented by the Desert Fathers.

The Monastery of St Catherine is located near the base of Mount Sinai and on the site of the biblical burning bush. Moses lived for forty years in this area, tending flocks of sheep and 'cleansing his soul in the silence and solitude of the Sinai Desert'.[14] Then, according to the book of Exodus, 'the angel of the Lord' appeared to Moses 'in a flame of fire out of the midst of a bush'. Although the 'bush burned with fire . . . the bush was not consumed'. God called to Moses 'out of the midst of the bush', told him that the place on which he stood was holy ground, and asked Moses to lead the children of Israel out of bondage in Egypt to the promised land of Canaan.

Because of the importance of the Sinai in biblical history, and because of the tranquil quality of the place, many early Christian monks came to the site of the burning bush. Originally they lived alone in caves, coming together only on holy days. However, in the sixth century Emperor Justinian ordered the building of a church and a walled monastic fortress at the site of the burning bush. The monastery became known as the Monastery of the Transfiguration, named after a beautiful mosaic of the transfiguration of Christ that was created by the monks and that symbolized the spiritual perfection to which the monks aspired.

It was renamed the Monastery of St Catherine several centuries later. During the persecution of Christians in the fourth century, St Catherine had 'confessed

THE MONASTERY OF ST CATHERINE.

ABOVE AND RIGHT: THE PYRAMID AT MAYDUM.

her faith in Jesus Christ and publicly accused the emperor of sacrificing to idols'. Her faith was so strong that, even while she was being tortured, she persuaded members of the emperor's family and others to convert to Christianity. After she was executed, her body vanished. It is said that angels transported it to the peak of the mountain in the Sinai that now bears her name. Three centuries later, monks from the Monastery of the Transfiguration, guided by a dream, climbed the mountain, found her body, and brought it to the church, where they placed it in a golden casket.[15]

The other principal sites illustrated here are some of the pyramids that are located in desert settings. I was particularly drawn to the pyramid at Maydum (also spelled Meidum or Maidum), about fifty miles south of Cairo. Relatively unknown and infrequently visited, the pyramid was started by King Huni in the third dynasty (approximately 2600 BC) and finished by his son Sneferu. A seven-stepped pyramid was built over a flat-roofed burial chamber. Subsequently an outer facing was added; however, much of the facing collapsed and now lies around the base of the pyramid.

Also illustrated are the great pyramids of Giza. As Cairo has grown, Giza has become much less tranquil than it used to be. Yet at dawn, watching the sun rise behind the pyramids, the visitor can still sense the timelessness of the place.

ABOVE: EARLY MORNING AT THE GREAT
HYPOSTYLE HALL, THE TEMPLE OF KARNAK, LUXOR.
RIGHT: THE PYRAMID OF CHEPHREN, GIZA.

MONUMENT VALLEY
Arizona & Utah · USA

Monument Valley is located on the border between Arizona and Utah in the southwestern United States. It is a semi-desert region where the combination of poor soil and limited rainfall makes life difficult for the few Navajo families who choose to live there.

Monument Valley is part of the Navajo reservation and is operated by the Navajos as a tribal park. Access is limited, and the single, poorly maintained dirt road into the valley makes each visit an adventure. However, once you are close to the spectacular scenery of the park, you begin to appreciate the reluctance of the Navajos to 'develop' the park. The visitor feels gratitude that the setting has been left relatively untouched, and, on looking around, it is easier to imagine a stagecoach coming into view than a modern automobile.

ABOVE: AGATHLA (OR AGATHLAN), A VOLCANIC
FORMATION NEAR THE ENTRANCE TO MONUMENT VALLEY.
LEFT: DAWN AT MONUMENT VALLEY.

WEST MITTEN AND FULL MOON.

The most popular sight is the view of 'the mittens' from the visitor center at the entrance to the valley. From there, visitors descend into the valley and drive around a loop road that includes most of the other best-known sites. I have also hired a Navajo guide to take me to more remote areas, and each occasion has been memorable – especially one morning when we started off in the dark, drove for an hour into the park, and then just watched and waited as the sky began to lighten and the rocks started to undergo magical color transformations. Eventually, the sun rose over the formations known as the 'totem pole' and *yei-bi-chei*, and the buttes and mesas around us turned a brilliant red that rivaled the color of Ayers Rock. During four wonderful hours, we never saw another human being.

Monument Valley is one of those places that seem familiar even to people who have never been there before. Possibly that is because the valley was used as the

EAST MITTEN AND JUNIPER.

setting for many western epics, including John Ford's *Stagecoach*. It has also been the setting for many advertisements seen on television or in magazines.

However, no matter how many times you have seen a picture of the major formations of Monument Valley, experiencing them in person is quite different. For me they invariably produce a silent exclamation of wonder and awe. It is the same overwhelming reaction that one feels in a great cathedral such as Chartres. At Monument Valley, the experience of beauty is even more intense because the setting is natural and because the experience changes continuously with the lighting and weather conditions. Back-lighting changes to front-lighting. Shadows lengthen and colors intensify. A puffy cloud appears almost on cue and poses over a butte or behind a weathered arch. Best of all, a sudden summer storm may blacken the sky and transform a peaceful scene into one that is angry and dramatic, with savage displays of power.

THE MITTENS IN LATE AFTERNOON.

STORM CLOUDS OVER MITCHELL BUTTE (ABOVE) CAST
A SHADOW ON MERRITT BUTTE (RIGHT).

ABOVE: THE SUN'S EYE, A FORMATION OF ERODED SANDSTONE.
RIGHT: THE TOTEM POLE AND YEI-BI-CHEI AT DAWN.
OVERLEAF: THE VIEW THROUGH THE NORTH WINDOW.

Part Two

CAVES

PLACES OF REBIRTH

Since prehistoric times, caves have been places of refuge — places to hide from danger, and to escape from wind, rain, or excessive heat. Caves have also had a symbolic significance. A cave is a dark, protected place, located in Mother Earth, and, upon entering a cave man is symbolically approaching the possibility of being reborn.

In earlier times, this rebirth took a literal form. Important people were laid to rest in caves with food and water to sustain them as they began another lifetime. The tumuli and grave barrows of neolithic man and the burial chambers of royalty in ancient Egypt are artificial caves of this type.

Prehistoric man also knew rebirth of a more symbolic nature — rebirth of the spirit, particularly through communion with animal spirits. The example used here is the cave-temple of France, where thousands of years ago prehistoric man descended into sanctuaries in the earth and created extraordinary works of art — paintings, engravings, and sculptures of animals.

For others, symbolic rebirth in a cave took place through meditation. Pictured here are the caves at Ajanta and Ellora, in India, the earliest of which were started in the second century BC by wandering Buddhist monks. In Turkey, the Cappadocia region became a place of refuge for early Christians who dug monastic cells in formations of soft volcanic ash.

Caves also have sinister connotations. Dragons, bears, and snakes live in caves. The devil and his domain (hell) are usually pictured as being in an underground cavern. When man goes into a cave, he enters the underworld; he has to deal with the demons — especially his own demons. In the darkness of a cave, he deals with his dark side.

Native Americans also understand the need to deal with all spirits, whether benevolent or not. Illustrated here are kivas (chambers in the earth that are entered from above by a ladder) used by the Anasazi between about AD 1000 and 1300. For the Anasazi, as well as for present-day Native Americans, the kiva was a place for sacred ceremony and for healings to be performed.

ROQUE ST-CHRISTOPHE, THE DORDOGNE, FRANCE.

THE CAVE-TEMPLES
OF FRANCE

At least seventy thousand years ago, prehistoric man inhabited large numbers of cliff dwellings and rock shelters in an area of southwestern France centered on the Vézère River. One of the dwellings is pictured here, the 'Roque St-Christophe', near Les Eyzies in the Dordogne. Its five terraces carved into the limestone cliff face extend a total length of more than two miles. It was continuously occupied from prehistoric times until four hundred years ago when, during the Wars of Religion, the Catholic king ordered the destruction of the dwellings, which had become a fortress for the Huguenots.

In the same area of France – and in northern Spain – are caves going deep into the earth. The caves, which have been called the 'birthplace of art', contain extraordinary paintings, engravings, and sculptures. The example used here is Lascaux, a few miles away from the Roque St-Christophe, near the town of Montignac. Lascaux was never lived in, and it is removed from the centers of prehistoric urban life. Around 15,000 BC, the artists who created Lascaux withdrew from their companions, entered the cave, and descended into the earth. Working in blackness relieved only by small lamps fueled by animal fat, they created startling visual panoramas, organized in content and accurate in detail. Their principal subjects were bulls, bison, cows, horses, goats, deer, and sometimes mammoths.

The work was sophisticated; for example, in some paintings the legs farthest from the viewer are slightly separated from the body of the animal to create an impression of depth. Other figures are surrounded by traces of white to give the sense of vitality.[1]

In many cases, natural features in the stone were incorporated into the design: a raised feature became an eye, a curved ridge became an underbelly or rump. It is as though the artist found the animal in the stone and brought out its features. The artist understood these animals, and, in painting them, he seems to have identified with them.

ROQUE ST-CHRISTOPHE.

The particular animals portrayed had symbolic significance, and there is little doubt that the creation of the art and the observation of it were religious acts – a religion centered on – and taking place in – Mother Earth, the creator of the bulls, the bison, the mammoths, and of man himself. The caverns were sanctuaries. Even today, going into these caves, passing through a narrow opening and emerging into a larger decorated cavern, evokes a sense of being in a great cathedral.² One chamber at Lascaux has been referred to as the Sistine Chapel of Prehistory.

One can only imagine what these temples would have been like in earlier times without the tour groups and with only the flickering light of the lamps. At first, the paintings would have been almost invisible. As one sat and focused on a wall, the features of an individual animal would have become more apparent. That figure would have led to another, and gradually one would have felt surrounded by the figures, in the center of a grand constellation both static and in movement.

The place where one gets this sense most clearly is probably Rouffignac, the 'Cave of the Hundred Mammoths', where the visitor rides a small train deeper and deeper into the earth. The headlamp of the train provides the only light, and one cannot see farther than a few feet ahead. Outcrops of rock are briefly illuminated and pass by into darkness.

The train continues for what seems like miles. At the end of the line one gets off the train and walks into a great chamber, overlooking an abyss, where the ceiling is decorated with paintings of mammoths, horses, bison, and ibex. One senses that only an urgent desire to 'go inside', both literally and figuratively, could have brought the artists to this place, and only inspiration and the need to transcend the artists' physical existence could have produced this art. As Joseph Campbell wrote:

'As in Chartres Cathedral the mystery of the hidden history of the universe is revealed through imagery of an anthropomorphic pantheon, so here, in these temple caves, the same mystery is made known through animal forms that are at once in movement and at rest. These forms are magical; midway, as it were, between the living species of the hunting plains and the universal ground of night, out of which the animals come, back into which they return, and which is the very substance of these caves.'³

LEFT: PAINTINGS AT LASCAUX II – 'TAUREAUX ET CHEVAUX' AND 'GRAND TAUREAU'.
(COURTESY DORDOGNE DEPT OFFICE OF TOURISM).
RIGHT: PREHISTORIC CAVE-DWELLING AT ROQUE ST-CHRISTOPHE.

THE CAVE-TEMPLES
OF INDIA

In the second century BC, a group of wandering Buddhist monks came to Ajanta (about two hundred miles northeast of Bombay). It is believed they were looking for a dry, safe place to meditate during the monsoon season. In the hillside above the river, they began to hollow out caves in the rock. Over the course of almost eight centuries, large numbers of monks and craftsmen created approximately thirty cave-temples, monasteries, and halls, with many beautiful frescoes and sculptures.

The caves are of two basic types: *chaityas* (sanctuaries or chapel-shrines), which were for worship, and *viharas* (monasteries, literally 'rainy season retreats'), which were principally for residence. The earlier caves were decorated simply, with Buddha never portrayed in human form but represented through

ABOVE: THE HINDU TEMPLE KAILASA AT ELLORA.
RIGHT: EARLY BUDDHIST CAVE TEMPLES AND MONASTERY, ELLORA.

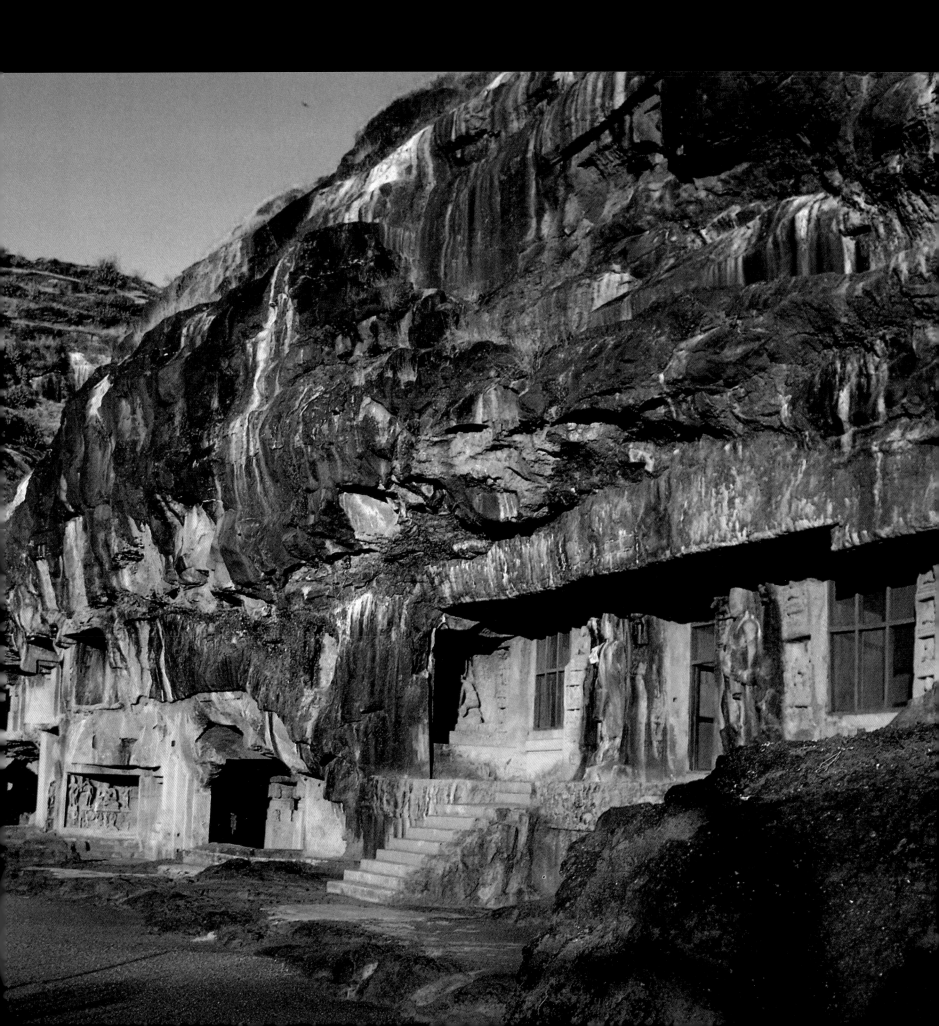

RAVANA SHAKING THE SACRED MOUNTAIN OF KAILAS; SHIVA STOPS
RAVANA BY SIMPLY PRESSING DOWN WITH ONE FOOT (CAVE 29).

symbols. The later caves are more ornate, with Buddha deified and portrayed in numerous postures, often surrounded by Bodhisattvas. The frescoes at Ajanta are particularly impressive, richly depicting dramatic scenes in the life of Buddha and the pageant of contemporary life.

In the sixth and seventh centuries AD, the focus shifted to Ellora (about seventy miles from Ajanta), where twelve Buddhist caves were created between about AD 550 and 750. These caves took much the same form as the caves at Ajanta, though the emphasis was less on painting and more on sculpture, with elaborate carved figures and scenes filling many of the walls. Particularly beautiful is a complex worship hall (cave 10) with a nave and two aisles, a carved shrine or 'stupa' at the back, and a vaulted 'timber' ceiling carved from stone. Nearby is a cave on three levels, with central meditation halls, side cells, and rich statuary, including two groups of seven seated Buddhas.

In addition to the Buddhist caves, Hindu cave-temples were created at Ellora between about AD 600 and 875, and Jain caves were carved from about AD 800 to 1000.[4] Thus sanctuaries of three major world religions can be seen located within a few feet of each other.

The most famous is the Hindu rock-temple, Kailasa, which has been called the greatest work of art in India. Its overall shape is modeled on Mount Kailas, the sacred mountain in Tibet.[5] Kailasa was excavated from the top by digging out deep vertical trenches into the hillside and then carving out of one solid rock a temple that is larger than the Parthenon. It is estimated that three million cubic feet of rock had to be chipped away to create Kailasa and that hundreds of craftsmen were employed in the work for more than a century. In addition to life-size carved elephants, the temple is filled with carved panels depicting events involving gods and goddesses, particularly Shiva. The main shrine contains the *yoni-linga*, the symbol of Shiva's creative powers.

A third important cave-temple complex is located on Elephanta Island in the harbor between the peninsula of Bombay and the mainland. It was excavated in the eighth century AD and was probably a private chapel for the royal family (the Rashtrakuta dynasty). The temple is dedicated to Shiva and contains a central shrine with *yoni-linga*, long rows of columns, and numerous panels showing Shiva in different forms.

Symbolically, it is important that Elephanta is approached from the sea, which, being in constant motion, represents unlimited life energy. 'On the human level, the sea is the mind, restless and creative, whose depths are the source of all thought and imagination. . . .'[6] In contrast, the island represents stability and a place of refuge – a tranquil spiritual center in a sea of chaos.[7]

The cave-temples at Ellora, Ajanta, and Elephanta are extraordinarily impressive. It is hard to imagine fully the dedication of the monks and craftsmen who created these sactuaries. At the same time, it is difficult today to experience the tranquility that those monks were seeking. This difficulty is a product of the concentration of people that inevitably occurs in any major tourist attraction involving a confined space; moreover, here, in addition to the tourists, there are large numbers of frustratingly persistent guides, guards, salesmen, and others seeking a little 'baksheesh'.

Solitude is difficult to attain but not impossible. For me, the best opportunities were at Ellora in some of the less popular caves, particularly the monasteries. There, in the late afternoon, with the sun slanting into the meditation halls, making its way across the stone floors, and illuminating bits of carvings on the innermost recesses, one gradually reclaims a sense of wonder, a sense of what motivated those monks. That realization has nothing to do with the statistics one hears on a tour about how long the work took or how much rock was carried away. It has to do not with the mind but with the emotions that manifest when sitting quietly in a sacred space created by inspired, loving hands.

ABOVE: A BUDDHIST CHAITYA HALL AT AJANTA, WITH 'TIMBERED'
CEILING CARVED FROM STONE (CAVE 19).
RIGHT: SEVEN STONE FIGURES OF BUDDHA ILLUMINATED BY LATE
AFTERNOON SUNLIGHT THAT PENETRATES THE INNER RECESSES
OF A THREE-STORY MONASTERY AT ELLORA (CAVE 12).

CAPPADOCIA

Turkey

Three per cent of Turkey is in Europe; the rest – Anatolia – is in Asia Minor. Mount Ararat in northeast Anatolia is where Noah's ark may have landed, and Catalhoyuk (south of Ankara), which dates from around 7000 BC, is one of the oldest communities on earth. Anatolia has always been a crossroads between Europe and Asia – Occident and Orient. It has been influenced by many cultures and has had a turbulent history. In addition to quarrels among tribes, Anatolia was occupied or invaded by, among others, Indo-European Hittites, Phrygians, Persians, Greeks, Macedonians, Egyptians, Gauls from Thrace, Romans, Crusaders, and Mongolians. During part of this time, and particularly during the early Christian period, the Cappadocian region was a place of refuge.

Cappadocia is a relatively small triangular area approximately one hundred and fifty miles southeast of Ankara. Frequent eruptions from two volcanoes covered much of the area with a thick layer of hot volcanic ash, which hardened into a soft, porous stone called 'tuff' or 'tufa'. Over thousands of years, erosion of the tuff by water and wind has created fantastic shapes. The best known of these are the 'fairy chimneys', pinnacles that are often capped by boulders of hard stone that protect the tuff beneath them from further erosion. Unusual colors, including ivory, yellow, blue-grey, and various shades of red, add to the other-worldly quality of the landscape.

In the fourth century AD, Cappadocia was the home of three Christian saints (Basil the Great, Gregory of Nazianus, and Gregory of Nyssa). It was an active center of Christian life and religious authority. St Basil recognized the value of both communal monasticism and a stricter asceticism. In the second half of the fourth century, a recluse in search of solitude carved a cave dwelling into the tuff, using only a stick as a digging tool. Others followed his lead, and soon large numbers of cells were carved into the soft rock. Occupants of the cells combined individual meditation with communal work in the fields. Over the years, rock

CHRISTIAN MONASTERY AT GOREME, CAPPADOCIA.

churches, chapels, and monasteries were also carved, especially in the area around Goreme. From the end of the fourth century until the beginning of the seventh, Cappadocia was a place of peace with a flourishing religious life.

The peace was shattered when the Persians invaded Anatolia. They reached Cappadocia by the middle of the seventh century. For the next two hundred years, Cappadocia was a frequent battleground in the Arab-Byzantine wars. The Arabs, carrying the 'True Cross', repeatedly attacked the Christians, who sought refuge in their cave dwellings. In order to survive they dug deep into the earth and constructed underground cities for up to sixty thousand people, hiding the entrances by covering them with large stones when the enemy approached. During the eighth and ninth centuries, the Arabs were not the only danger to the Christian communities, as large numbers of Christians were killed during the great massacres of the iconoclastic period in which religious images were destroyed wholesale.

In 843, relative peace returned under Empress Theodora. With the peace came the revitalization of above-ground church construction, the restoration of destroyed churches, and the flourishing of ecclesiastical art. Simple geometric designs applied to rock walls and ceilings in early churches evolved into elaborate, multi-color frescoes painted on plaster. By the eleventh century the hollowing out of rocks for religious retreats had reached its peak, though Christian communities continued to exist in the rocks of Cappadocia until the twentieth century.

Ironically, it was recently discovered that some of the rocks that had provided shelter to the persecuted for hundreds of years were themselves the source of great danger. The rock in the area around Karain was found to cause a certain type of cancer, and the villagers were evacuated. Today, the majority of the rock dwellings are unoccupied, with the fairy chimneys and other formations standing as silent sentinels in an eerie yet tranquil landscape.

FAIRY CHIMNEYS NEAR URGUP.

ERODED FORMATIONS AT GOREME.
OVERLEAF: FRESCOES IN TWO CHURCHES
CARVED INTO THE ROCK AT GOREME.
ST BARBARA (LEFT) AND ELMALI 'THE
APPLE CHURCH' (RIGHT).

GOREME VALLEY.

THE NATIVE AMERICAN KIVA

Colorado & New Mexico · USA

Around two thousand years ago, a group of Native Americans began to develop a center of civilization in the area of the United States now called the Four Corners (where the states of Arizona, New Mexico, Utah, and Colorado all meet). We know them as the Anasazi, a Navajo term meaning the 'Ancient Ones' or the 'Ancient Enemy'. The Anasazi gradually changed from being nomadic hunter-gatherers to having a highly socialized life in villages and towns. Between about AD 1000 and 1300, they created their most enduring monuments, the cliff dwellings at Mesa Verde in Colorado and the great pueblos of Chaco Canyon in New Mexico. There, as at their other principal location (Kayenta, Arizona), the centers of community life were the underground chambers now known as *kivas*.

MESA VERDE, COLORADO. ABOVE: SMALL KIVA
AT 'SPRUCE TREE HOUSE'. LEFT: THE 'CLIFF PALACE'.

RESTORED 'GREAT KIVA' AT AZTEC RUINS NATIONAL MONUMENT, NEW MEXICO.

'Kiva' is a Hopi word; the Hopis (and other current Pueblo Indians) are thought to be direct descendants of the Anasazi, and the kiva is the strongest physical link between the Pueblo Indians and their ancestors. Generally round or rectangular, a kiva is sunk deep in the ground, like the womb of Mother Earth.

Everything about the kiva is symbolic. A small hole in the floor (the *sipapu* or *sipapuni*) represents 'the umbilical cord leading from Mother Earth', as well as the 'path of man's emergence from the previous . . . world'.[8] Entry to the kiva is by a ladder, which serves as another sipapu to the present world above the kiva. The emergence is symbolically enacted in a ceremony at which 'initiates undergo spiritual rebirth'.[9]

Kivas were and are sacred places used for rituals and ceremonies. Healings are performed there and prayers are offered. Ceremonies of the ancient ones probably revolved around the seasonal cycle – 'renewal and rebirth at the winter solstice, fertility and growth in the spring, rain during the summer, and thanksgiving in the fall'.[10]

Because they are the focal point of prayer and ceremony, kivas have been compared to churches. Yet, as Frank Waters has pointed out, the architecture of the kiva, like many of the concepts underlying the ceremonies, is very different from that of the European church:

'The Christian church is built above ground, its phallic steeple thrusting into the sky; the kiva is built below ground, a womb of Mother Earth. Inside the Christian church, altar and priests are raised above the level of common worshipers and adorned with the richest vestments; while in the kiva, altar and priests occupy the lowest level, where the priests are always barefoot to show their humility.'[11]

Mesa Verde, now a national park, was occupied by the Anasazi for about seven hundred years, beginning around AD 600. There they built complex stone villages in the protected recesses of canyon walls. Many spectacular cliff dwellings still remain, sheltered from the weather by the overhanging cliffs. The place called Spruce Tree House had 114 rooms and eight kivas and probably housed more than a hundred people. Cliff Palace and Long House were even larger, the former including over two hundred rooms and twenty-three kivas. Today most of the kivas at Mesa Verde are missing their roofs, which were supported by logs that deteriorated over the centuries. However, two kiva roofs at Spruce Tree House have been restored, and it is possible for visitors to enter one today by a ladder from above, just as the Anasazi did.

The desert country of Chaco Canyon, with difficult growing conditions and marginal rainfall, and an unlikely place for the center of a civilization. Yet it was home to at least two thousand Anasazi and was a focal point of spiritual activity, connected to other Anasazi settlements by a far-reaching network of roads. Within Chaco Canyon, Pueblo Bonito (the 'pretty village') contained six hundred rooms and forty kivas; Chetro Ketl was almost as large. Casa Rinconada (literally 'House in a Box Canyon'), built around AD 1100, measures sixty-four feet in diameter and is one of the largest 'great kivas' in the southwest.

WALL OF CASA RINCONADA, A GREAT KIVA AT CHADO CANYON, NEW MEXICO.

Part Three

MOUNTAINS

ABODE OF THE GODS

The Greek Gods lived on Mount Olympus. In other cultures, too, mountains have been regarded as, if not the actual home of the gods, at least the connection between heaven and earth. Man went to the mountains to make contact with the divine. The transfiguration of Christ occurred on top of a mountain; Moses received the Ten Commandments on Mount Sinai; Gabriel appeared to Muhammad on a mountain; God spoke to Abraham on a mountain; and certain revelations to Buddha are also associated with mountains.[1]

More symbolically, because mountains 'reach up from the earth towards the sky', they 'are symbols of the ascent from the earthly plane to the spiritual'.[2] They are uplifting to the spirit.

Mountains continue to be viewed as places to receive divine inspiration. They are 'emblems of the stable and eternal'.[3] They are places to experience nature at its most awesome and spectacular, and thereby to achieve a different perspective on man's importance or on the relative insignificance of day-to-day problems. On a physical plane, they are places at which to be stimulated by the pure air, the clarity of the light, the panoramic views, and the silence of the heights.

Illustrated here are: the Himalayas of Nepal, containing the world's tallest peaks and several of the mountains most sacred to Hindus, Buddhists, and Jains; Mount Sinai, the location of God's revelation to Moses; the volcanic mountains of Bali, which to the Balinese are synonymous with holiness. and purity; the Alps of France, Italy, and Switzerland; and Mount Rainier, a peak in the Cascade Range of Washington State that was sacred to the Native Americans of that area.

LES DRUS, NEAR MONT BLANC, FRANCE.

THE HIMALAYAS OF NEPAL

The word 'Himalayas' means 'abode of the snows'. It is no wonder that the Himalayas have also been called the 'abode of the gods'. Its peaks are the tallest on earth, the closest that man can ascend to the heavens.

Many sacred mountains are in the Himalayas. Mount Kailas in Tibet is thought by Hindus to be the throne of Shiva, where he sits in perpetual meditation with his consort Parvati, the daughter of Himalaya. Kailas is also venerated by Buddhists, Jains, and the Tibetan Bons. It is thought to be the center of both the earth and the universe, the 'conceptual point where sacred reality impinges upon profane reality, where time and eternity meet, and where all dualities are resolved'.[4] It is a place 'where spiritual transformation is possible'.[5]

Nandi Devi is in northern India, close to Tibet. It is surrounded by almost seventy peaks, forming a protective wall of rock and ice. According to legend, its name comes from Princess Nanda who, fleeing her father's killers, took refuge on the mountain and became one with it.[6]

ABOVE: SUNRISE OVER DORJE LAKPA AND GYALZEN FROM NAGARKOT.
LEFT: LOOKING TOWARD MACHHAPUCHHARE AND THE ANNAPURNA RANGE FROM NEAR POKHARA, NEPAL.

In Nepal, the government has recognized the sacred nature of Machhapuch-hare (the 'fish tail mountain') and Gauri-Shankar, and it is forbidden to climb them. The reasoning is that scaling a mountain peak connotes conquering the mountain, the mastery of man over nature. Yet in the case of a sacred peak, it is felt that the attitude should be one of worship, of opening oneself to the mountain.[7] As Lama Govinda wrote, 'Instead of conquering it, the religious-minded man prefers to be conquered by the mountain. . . . To him the mountain is a divine symbol, and as little as he would put his foot upon a sacred image, so little would he dare to put his foot on the summit of a sacred mountain.'[8] He added that 'to see the greatness of a mountain, one must keep one's distance; to understand its form, one must move around it; to experience its moods, one must see it at sunrise and sunset, at noon and at midnight, in sun and in rain, in snow and in storm, in summer and in winter and in all the other seasons.'[9]

Eight of the fourteen tallest peaks in the world are in Nepal, including Mount Everest. Though they can be seen from afar, approaching them requires a considerable journey by foot. By making a personal step-by-step effort to advance toward a distant mountain, one achieves a perspective of humility, awe, and openness of heart, facilitating the full experience of the majesty of the mountains, the special quality of light at higher altitudes, and the stillness of a place far removed from civilization. In Nepal, most treks are of one to four weeks' duration; however, a 'mini-trek' to the top of a lower peak can also provide a sense of these qualities, as well as a panoramic view of the taller mountains. Even from the valleys, the sight of the last rays of afternoon sunlight on the mountaintops can be a deeply moving experience.

To the pilgrim, the person making both an external and internal spiritual journey, the experience is especially intense. As Lama Govinda wrote after a pilgrimage to Mount Kailas, the view of a sacred mountain is one of the most inspiring on earth:

'[It is] a view, indeed, which makes the beholder wonder about whether it is one of this world or a dreamlike vision of the next. An immense peace lies over this landscape and fills the heart of the pilgrim, making him immune to all personal concerns, because, as in a dream, he feels one with his vision.'[10]

EVEREST, LHOTSE, AND MAKALU FROM THE AIR.
OVERLEAF: MACHHAPUCHHARE (LEFT) AND ANNAPURNA III (RIGHT)

ABOVE: STUPAS AT BODHNATH AND SWAYAMBHUNATH (RIGHT),
WITH GILDED PINNACLES, PRAYER FLAGS AND BUDDHA'S ALL-SEEING EYES.
PRECEDING PAGES: ANNAPURNA IV AND II, FROM POKHARA.

MOUNT SINAI

Egypt

Mount Sinai is known by many names, including Gabal Musa (in Arabic), Mount Moses, Mount Horeb, and the Holy Peak. It is the mountain where Moses is thought to have received the 'tablets of the law' with the Ten Commandments.

As the story was told in the book of Exodus, when Moses led the children of Israel out of Egypt into the wilderness, they stopped at the base of Mount Sinai. 'The Lord came down upon Mount Sinai, to the top of the mountain; and the Lord called to Moses at the top of the mountain and Moses went up.' '[A] cloud covered the mount', and 'the glory of the Lord abode on Mount Sinai'. Moses went into the cloud and was on the mountain forty days and forty nights. When the Lord finished communing with Moses, he gave Moses 'two tables [tablets] of testimony, tables of stone, written with the finger of God', so that Moses could instruct the children of Israel.

Moses is recognized as a prophet by followers of Islam, as well as Christianity and Judaism, so Mount Sinai is revered by all those religions as the site of God's great revelation. It has been a place of pilgrimage since the early Christian era, and both a small mosque and a chapel (built over the remains of an ancient basilica) are located on the summit.

Despite its isolation and the barren character of the setting, Mount Sinai continues to attract large numbers of visitors, many of whom want the experience of climbing the mountain. The act of climbing Mount Sinai (unlike some other holy mountains) is not generally regarded as sacrilegious; indeed, most of those climbing Mount Sinai seem to do so with considerable respect for the mountain and with some feeling that their effort is part of their spiritual journey.

The summit is more than seven thousand feet above sea level and the ascent takes from two to three hours. The most direct ascent is by a route that includes over three thousand steps carved into the mountainside hundreds of years ago by

THE VIEW TO THE WEST FROM THE TOP OF MOUNT SINAI AT SUNRISE.

monks from the Monastery of St Catherine; the easier way is by a winding path that joins with the steps about two-thirds of the way up the mountain.

Like most climbers, I started at night, so that I could be on top at sunrise. The air was cool and still, and I felt I had never seen stars so clearly or in such quantity as at that moment. My small light illuminated only the next few steps. After a particularly steep hill, I paused to catch my breath; I looked back down the trail and saw two lights far below, making me feel good about my progress and reinforcing my determination to continue.

The last part of the climb involved more than seven hundred steps that seemed to go almost straight up. On reaching the top, I walked to the east side of the chapel, stepping over several people in sleeping bags. The sky was beginning to lighten, and I sat on a ledge to wait for the dawn. Soon I could make out the shapes of other peaks. There were layers of ridges and hills, dark blue close up and pale blue-grey in the distance. Eventually, a red glow appeared near the horizon, and a few minutes later the sun finally rose above some low clouds. On the west side of the mountain, the light of the sun warmed a hillside that was like nothing I had ever seen – fantastically shaped granite boulders with no vegetation whatsoever.

When I started down, I saw for the first time the steep trail I had climbed a few hours earlier and the sheer rock walls. I felt the intensity of the desert sun and was grateful that I had made the climb at night rather than in the heat of the day. The descent went quickly, and, as I neared the end, I reflected on what I had seen and on the significance of the place. It was a deeply satisfying experience.

THE CAMEL PATH USED TO ASCEND MOUNT SINAI.

ABOVE: THE MOON AND STARS PROVIDE ILLUMINATION FOR THOSE WHO CLIMB THE MOUNTAIN AT NIGHT.
RIGHT: HIKERS DESCENDING THROUGH A DEEP CLEFT IN THE ROCK.

THE SACRED MOUNTAINS OF BALI

Indonesia

In the late twentieth century, the island of Bali has come to symbolize the same ideal that Tahiti represented in the early nineteenth century: an idyllic place with beautiful beaches, happy people, tropical flowers, and lush scenery – a paradise on earth. Recently, however, like Tahiti before it, Bali has been altered by development and the commercial pressures of tourism. Yet Bali has a far better chance of retaining its unique character than the unfortunate island of Tahiti.

One reason has to do with the Balinese religion and the cultural depth of its people. Although Indonesia is a Muslim country, Bali is overwhelmingly Hindu. Its form of Hinduism (Hindu Dharma) is unique, having deep roots in animism and having absorbed elements of Mahayanic Buddhism, orthodox Shivaism,

ABOVE: PURA BESAKIH, THE MOTHER TEMPLE.
LEFT: GUNUNG AGUNG, THE MOST SACRED MOUNTAIN IN BALI.

tantric beliefs, and Javanized Hinduism.[11] Animism and the worship of nature spirits still lie at the core of its religious life. As a Covarrhubias wrote, 'Hinduism was simply an addition to the native religion – a strong but superficial veneer of decorative Hindu practice over a deeply rooted animism.'[12] The religion permeates the culture, and the Balinese culture affects all aspects of the life of a Balinese, including 'his work, his social involvements . . . and his artistic self-fulfillment'.[13]

For the Balinese, the world is separated into three parts: the higher world or world of the mountains; the middle world or world of the land; and the lower world or world of the seas.[14] Mountains are the home of the gods and are synonymous with sacredness and purity. The supreme god lives in the heavens above Gunung Agung, the holiest mountain and the 'navel of the world'. Half-way up the mountain is Bali's most sacred spot, Pura Besakih or the 'mother temple', which dates back to the eighth century. Mount Agung is the principal point of reference all over the island, and in every village there is a temple dedicated to the mountain. From any location, the direction toward the mountain is the Balinese word *kaja*, meaning 'sacred'.[15]

Mount Agung is a volcanic mountain and is literally the source of both life and death. In 1963 the volcano erupted, sending out showers of ash and streams of lava that destroyed much of eastern Bali. Pura Besakih was in the path of the lava, but the flow seemed to divide at the holy place, leaving the temple complex relatively unscathed. Many Balinese interpreted the eruption as symbolic, as 'divine retribution for the past sins of the people'.[16] Some of those in the path of the lava accepted the calamity with a fatalistic attitude, simply waiting for the deities to determine whether to spare their lives or to kill them.

A second sacred mountain is Gunung Batur, a volcanic cone inside a larger volcano that has a rim approximately seven miles in diameter. A road runs along the rim, providing spectacular views. Inside the rim, at the base of Mount Batur is a lake, next to huge lava fields and ridges. A hot spring affords refreshing relaxation for hikers who undertake the steep five-hour hike to the top of Mount Batur and back.

Mount Batur's temple (Ulun Danu Batur) is another of the most sacred places in Bali. Off the route of tour buses, the temple has a vibrant life, especially on festival days, and is the focal point for the villages around Kintamani.

GUNUNG BATUR BECOMING VISIBLE THROUGH EARLY MORNING FOG.

ABOVE AND RIGHT: THE TEMPLE OF ULUN DANU BATUR, ON THE
RIM OF AN ANCIENT VOLCANO.

MONT BLANC AND THE MATTERHORN

France · Italy · Switzerland

The Alps cover parts of France, Italy, Switzerland, and Austria. Europe's tallest mountains, the Alps include beautiful countryside, as well as spectacular peaks and glaciers.

The Alps are another location where, at one time, man apparently lived at peace with his surroundings. The mountains, the trees, rocks, and springs were respected as sacred places.[17] Something happened to change that. By the 1800s, natives of the region 'spoke of a ruined city on [the] summit [of the Matterhorn] where spirits dwelt.... To them the mountains were to be feared and suspected as haunts of monsters, wizards and crabbed goblins – and the devil.'[18] They spoke of a purgatory of ice, a place of eternal snow.[19] The mountains were referred to as the 'montagnes maudites', or accursed mountains; they were the abode of evil spirits.

To some extent, the fears of the natives were understandable. Villages encircled by mountains were continually threatened by avalanches and glaciers. The people associated the mountains with cold, snow, and famine.[20] Yet the

ABOVE: THE MATTERHORN FROM ZERMATT.
LEFT: MONT BLANC FROM NEAR CHAMONIX.

feelings about the mountains also reflected a change of perspective. People were no longer living as part of nature; nature was now the opposition.

The legends began to die out after the first successful ascent of Mont Blanc in 1786, though for many years the high mountains were visited only by climbers and by those who collected crystals from the upper reaches. Today of course the Alps are popular for skiing in the winter and hiking and mountaineering in the summer. To the cynical, the principal relationship between the inhabitants and nature appears to be one of economic exploitation. In the popular resort towns it seems that chalets, hotels, and restaurants for visitors are being constructed on every square inch of land.

Pictured here are the areas around Mont Blanc (France/Italy) and the Matterhorn (Switzerland/Italy). The two mountains provide a contrast in styles. Mont Blanc, the tallest mountain in Europe, has an undistinguished profile. It can be quite easily identified from far away; from nearby, it tends to be obscured by its smaller neighbors. The Matterhorn stands out from close up, as a result of its distinctive profile and its isolation from other mountains in the range. No natural landmark in Europe is more instantly recognizable than the Matterhorn, and no other mountain so dominates the view from the valley below.

The Alps are included in this book because of the contemplative pursuits that are possible in this magnificent landscape – for example, sitting quietly by a rushing mountain stream, looking out toward a snow-covered peak, or walking through an evergreen forest with mountains in the background, hearing the sounds of water and birds. These are the times when one's problems disappear, or at least seem less important, and when new thoughts come to the surface.

Despite the popularity of the Alps, they continue to have a strong spiritual effect on people. One morning I took the cog railway from Zermatt to the Gornergrat. The railway stops at an altitude of about ten thousand feet, far above the tree-line, at a location that affords superb views of the Matterhorn and the surrounding peaks.

As I watched, a group of American visitors spontaneously started singing the Christian hymn, 'Nearer My God To Thee'. When they finished, they joked that they were as close to God as they hoped to be for many years. The moment was humorous but also indicative of the way people feel in the presence of a great mountain – humble and very much aware of their connection with the divine.

VALLÉE BLANCHE FROM AIGUILLE DU MIDI.

ABOVE: MONT BLANC AND THE GLACIER DES BOSSONS.
LEFT: AIGUILLE LES DRUS.

MONT BLANC AT SUNRISE.

THE MATTERHORN AT SUNRISE.

MOUNT RAINIER
Washington State · USA

Mount Rainier, a dormant volcanic cone, is the tallest peak in the Cascade Range in the Pacific northwest of the United States. Dwarfing its neighbors, Rainier can be seen for nearly a hundred miles in most directions.

Twenty-seven glaciers, covering more than forty square miles, flank the mountain and feed rivers below. Subalpine meadows provide colorful displays – wild flowers in summer and huckleberries and mountain ash in autumn. Lakes are surrounded by forests of fir and hemlock. Animals range from tiny pika to elk, bear, and cougar.

The most popular area is named Paradise Valley;[21] the Native Americans called it Saghalie Illahe, meaning 'heavenly place' or 'land of peace'. To them 'it was a land where the soul was freed of the pressures and strife of the world below'.[22] Paradise Valley may seem less peaceful now, as a result of its popularity. But Mount Rainier National Park is large (378 square miles) and it is not difficult to find solitude amid its spectacular scenery. Indeed, at Rainier the variety of options makes it hard to decide what to choose – glaciers above the timber line, streams and waterfalls, meadows with intense colors and textures, clear lakes that reflect the mountain, or dense evergreen forests with cushioned trails and occasional shafts of sunlight penetrating the multiple layers of branches.

Rainier is the name given to the mountain in 1792 by Captain George Vancouver of the British navy, in honor of Rear-Admiral Peter Rainier. The Native American name is Ta-ho-ma (or Takhoma), and the mountain has been used by Native Americans since around 6000 BC for hunting, berry gathering, and ceremony. For them, the mountain was sacred and not to be violated by climbing. It was an enchanted mountain and an evil spirit was said to live in a fiery lake on the summit. Anyone reaching the summit would be seized by the demon, killed, and thrown into the lake.[23]

In another legend, a positive spirit living on the summit was angered by all the

MOUNT RAINIER REFLECTED IN TIPSOO LAKE AT SUNRISE.

ABOVE: DAWN AT TIPSOO LAKE. RIGHT: REFLECTION LAKE.

bad things he saw happening on the earth. He instructed a wise man to construct a long rope of arrows from the top of the mountain down to the foothills. He then directed good people and good animals to climb the rope. When they were safe, the spirit caused heavy rain to fall. Flood waters rose, destroying all the bad creatures. Once the flood subsided, the good people and animals descended from the mountain and repopulated the earth.[24]

In addition to Native Americans, later visitors have also been affected by the strong presence of the mountain. It has been called the 'Saint Peter's of the skies', and the 'greater and grander Olympus'. American naturalist John Muir found the view from the top unsurpassed 'in sublimity and grandeur'. The view from the base was equally inspiring; Muir described the mountain as 'awful in bulk and majesty', yet 'so fine and beautiful it might well fire the dullest observer to desperate enthusiasm'.

Tumtum Peak – Morning.

TUMTUM PEAK – BEFORE SUNSET.

HUCKLEBERRY BUSHES IN THEIR FALL COLORS.

ABOVE LEFT: NARADA FALLS.
ABOVE RIGHT: SUNLIGHT PENETRATING AN EVERGREEN FOREST,
MOUNT RAINIER NATIONAL PARK.

Part Four

SEACOASTS

RETURN TO SOURCE

THE BIG SUR COAST FROM NEAR PARTINGTON POINT, CALIFORNIA.

All life came from the sea, and, in returning to it, the individual is returning to his source. The sea seems endless in every direction. It is constantly in motion and in transition; facing the sea, an individual faces the elemental forces, the unknown, and the inevitability of change. The power of the sea and its psychological connection with the unconscious make us aware both of our fears and of our need to overcome them and find out what lies beneath the surface. The sea is also 'a shrine for the renewal of the tired spirit, . . . the source of the rejuvenating power of the eternal mother, . . . the infinite well of creativity.'[1]

In addition, for me the sea is a reminder of the importance of flexibility. Its waters adapt to the shape of any object they contact but have the power over time to wear down even the hardest rock. Supple sea plants that do not resist tidal movements seem to fare better against the sea than rigid objects. The same is true in our own lives; flexibility allows us to deal with the ebb and flow of life in a positive way, whereas rigidity makes much of life seem a struggle.

The examples illustrated begin with two open-air megalithic sanctuaries of prehistoric man located on seacoasts. These are followed by: the coast of Bali; Milford Sound, a fiord in New Zealand; two inspirational settings in Hawaii – the Kalalau Valley or 'Valley of Refuge' on Kauai, and Pu'uhonua-O-Honaunau; and the dramatic coastline of Big Sur in California. Finally, an example is included of a junction of land and river, rather than land and sea – the Ganges at Varanasi (or Benares), the most sacred place of pilgrimage for Hindus. Although pilgrimage sites tend not to be places of solitude, they also involve quests for inner peace, and even the most popular location may be regarded as a 'place of inspiration' if it facilitates quiet contemplation.

THE MEGALITHS
OF CARNAC
France

Carnac, the seaside resort on the south coast of Brittany in France, has been called the supermarket of the Druids. It contains an amazing wealth of standing stones, dolmens, and other forms of burial mounds, and may be the most important prehistoric site in Europe.

The megalith-building period[3] in northwest Europe began around 5000 BC and lasted for at least three thousand years. The standing stones are found in rows (alignments), in circles, and as large single stones. In some cases, they appear to be aligned to mark the cycles of sun and moon.[3] There are those who believe they even made possible the prediction of solar eclipses.

Beyond their astronomical significance, which would have been extremely valuable in determining when to plant crops and when to harvest, it appears that the stones were used in ceremony and ritual. It has also been suggested that the shapes of the stones and the tombs are symbolic, that they may represent reproductive organs, and that they were an aspect of a natural religion having to do with fertility rites related to the birth of animals and the sprouting of crops.

Much later, Christian crosses were placed on top of many of the stones, and a Christian church was built above the largest burial mound.

At one time there may have been as many as ten thousand standing stones at Carnac. It is thought that the Roman legions used many of the stones to build roads. Later road builders used them, as did canal builders.[4] Farmers also removed them to make room for their crops. Nonetheless, approximately 2500 standing stones can still be seen at Carnac, a concentration of magaliths that is without equal.

The three principal alignments of standing stones are north of the village at Le Menec, Kermario, and Kerlescan. At Le Menec, almost 1100 stones in twelve rows extend to the northeast for over half a mile. The majority of the stones are about three feet high, but at one end of the rows they average almost ten feet.

LE MENEC ALIGNMENTS AT CARNAC.

The alignment at Kermario is similar, with over a thousand stones remaining in seven rows. The one at Kerlescan is smaller, with several hundred stones in fan-shaped lines and a barrel-shaped arrangement of thirty-nine stones.[5]

Carnac is a popular vacation resort, and the three main alignments are adjacent to public roads. As a result, for much of the day the quantity of visitors tends to make contemplation difficult. However, there are many other standing stones and dolmens that can be reached on foot, and the sheer number of stones near Carnac means that quiet is assured at many of them. Even at Le Menec, Kermario and Kerlescan, the end of the day (and especially the time around dawn) is peaceful, and it is often possible to lose oneself in the monuments.

For me, one dawn spent at the alignments was among the most intense experiences I had in the course of preparing this book. Thick ground fog obscured the view. The houses and power lines that have been built near the stones were invisible. In each direction I could see only the closest two or three megaliths, seeming to rise out of the fog and tower over me. There was no sun to define their contours, but lichens and moss on the stones, and flowering gorse underneath, provided a colorful scene.

The stones are memorable at any time, but, on that day in the fog and dim light, they were mysterious and haunting. It could have been several thousand years ago, and my mind was filled with thoughts of earlier peoples and earlier times among the stones. No one else was around, and the stones had a powerful presence. I found myself attracted to certain stones and stood admiring their shapes and placing my hands on them.

Gradually, the sun began to burn through the fog. The appearance of the sun, rising between the stones, seemed particularly appropriate in a setting constructed by people for whom the daily birth and death of the sun probably lay at the core of their religious beliefs.

The Kermario alignments of standing stones.

ABOVE AND RIGHT: STONES AT KERMARIO.

THE STANDING STONES
OF CALLANISH
Scotland

Lewis is an island off the northwest coast of Scotland. Getting there generally involves flying, followed by a long drive and a three and one-half hour ferry ride. Once on Lewis, a short drive along peat bogs and moorland, with thousands of sheep but very few humans, brings you within sight of the standing stones of Callanish.

The Gaelic name that is applied to Callanish means 'place of pilgrimage'.[6] In the area of Callanish, there are twelve circles or other configurations of standing stones. The main group of stones is on top of a hill that overlooks an arm of the sea. Thirteen stones form a slightly flattened circle, near the center of which stands a stone almost sixteen feet tall. It is believed that these stones were erected as much as five thousand years ago.[7]

Some time later, a small crypt was placed in the ring, after which lines of stones were added in roughly east-west and north-south orientations. The totality (fifty-four standing stones) resembles a Celtic cross, although all of the stones at Callanish were erected long before the Christian era.

The stones are of gneiss, a coarse-grained, layered rock resembling granite. Individually, they have wonderful patterns, textures, and colors, and they are beautiful pieces of sculpture that make the work of many twentieth-century artists seem derivative and second rate. The overall color is grey, but from close up the colors range from white to black, with striations of salmon pink, olive, and even lavender. Some of the stones seem almost magnetic; you find yourself reaching out to touch them and feel the textures and contours.

Around the stones is a low fence; beyond are hillsides of grasses and heather. Much of the time, gale-force winds blow off the sea, making Callanish a bleak, bone-chilling place. The main circle is exposed to the elements, and often visitors use the stones as windbreaks to protect them from the strongest blasts. The fierce winds remind one forcibly of the challenges faced by the early residents of the area.

THE MAIN CIRCLE OF STONES AT CALLANISH.

THE EAST ROW OF STONES, WITH EAST LOCH ROAG (AN ARM
OF THE SEA) IN THE BACKGROUND.

The weather changes quickly in Scotland, and, even on the gloomiest day, an opening may appear in the clouds and shafts of light may come through – light of an incredible intensity that seems unique to northern locations. (On the other hand, the light may never appear, and, as I learned, anyone waiting for light to pierce the clouds had better have a good book to read, a dry place to sit, and considerable patience.)

Stonehenge and Callanish are possibly the most important groups of standing stones in Great Britain. Although their mysteries will never be fully revealed, both are believed to be, among other things, astronomical observatories. Stonehenge is related primarily to the movements of the sun and particularly to the solstices. Callanish also has its solar significance: the midsummer sunset occurs on the alignment from the group of stones known as Callanish IV to the main site, and the midwinter sunrise occurs in the reverse direction.

The principal alignments at Callanish, however, relate to the moon.[8] Callanish's latitude is such that when the moon rises at its southern maximum (every 18.6 years), it rises over the horizon for only a few minutes on one particular day. One avenue is so aligned that on that occasion the moon rises directly at the end of the avenue. It is also believed that the astronomer-priests at Callanish observed the link between the moon and the tides, and that they even may have been capable of predicting lunar eclipses.

The whole area of Callanish may have been a sacred area that ordinary people could enter only on certain days. It seems probable that Callanish was a place of worship, and possibly a place for sacrifice, as well as a meeting-place for the elders. It was certainly a special place, and it remains so today.

Some people come for a quick look and head off for one of the other sights on the island (or to stock up on Harris tweeds). Others feel drawn to Callanish and stay for literally weeks at a time. I spent three days close to the stones. Most of the time it rained heavily and the wind was at gale force. Nonetheless, the stones seemed the place to be. On the wet days, I tended to see each stone clearly and focused on the area immediately around me. On the dry days (or, more accurately, during the brief dry periods), I saw the stones more in the context of their environment – as the central feature of a landscape with grasses, hills, sky, and clouds. Either way, Callanish, with its ancient secrets and its strong presence, captures and holds the attention and the imagination.

ABOVE: DETAIL OF THE COLORS AND TEXTURES OF THE STONE.
LEFT: THE MAIN CIRCLE IN LATE AFTERNOON SUNLIGHT.

THE COAST OF BALI

Indonesia

In Bali, while the direction toward the holy mountains is called *kaja*, meaning 'sacred', the direction away from the mountains and toward the sea is called *kelod*, meaning 'profane'. The mountains are the homes of the deities and are synonymous with purity, whereas the seas are the home of demons and monsters. Yet even the bad Balinese spirits command respect and have to be dealt with; as a result, a number of important sea temples were constructed on cliffs or rock promontories, facing the sea.

The best known spot in Bali – and possibly the most photographed – is Tanah Lot on the southwest coast. Tanah Lot is a small sanctuary constructed on a large black rock at the edge of the Indonesian Ocean. From a location near the temple, visitors can watch the sun set over the sea, with the temple and rock in silhouette. Tanah Lot is extremely popular, and visitors are not likely to find themselves alone.

Equally picturesque, and more peaceful, is Ulu Watu on the western edge of the peninsula south of Denpasar. The temple was built around AD 976 and was the place where in earlier times a well-known priest was released from the cycle of life and death. It is often used today by mystics for meditation. The temple is on a cliff about one hundred and fifty feet above the water, and it provides a wonderful vantage point for sitting quietly at the end of the day and watching as the rocky cliffs turn to gold and the setting sun gradually changes the color of sea and sky to soft pastel hues.

SUNSET OVER THE OCEAN, FROM ULU WATU TEMPLE.

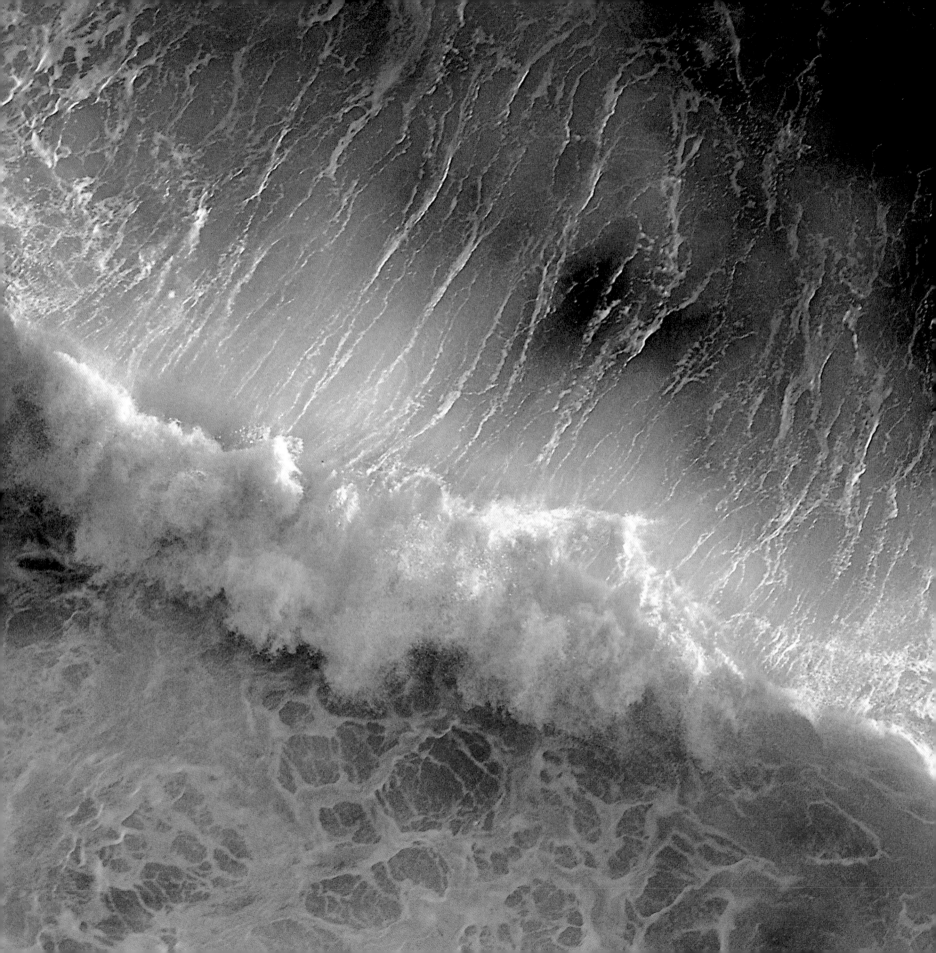

THE WESTERN COAST OF THE BUKIT BADUNG PENINSULA, FROM ULU WATU TEMPLE.

Above: The temple at Tanah Lot.
Right: Sunset at Ulu Watu.

MILFORD SOUND
New Zealand

Milford Sound in Fiordland National Park on the South Island of New Zealand is one of the most spectacular places on earth. Though termed a sound, Milford is a true fiord – a narrow inlet of the sea that was formed by glaciers. The mouth is relatively shallow, but, inside the sound, the water is up to twelve hundred feet deep.

Mountains rise almost straight up out of the water. Mitre Peak, which dominates the view of Milford Sound, stands more than a mile above the water. At dozens of points, water from springs and melting snow tumbles over the rocks and drops hundreds of feet into the sound.

Seals, dolphins, and crested penguins are frequent visitors, and crayfish are found in abundance at the mouth of the sound. Birds range from finches to white herons, and include falcons and mountain parrots. A few feet from the water a rain forest begins, a dark tangle of ferns, vines, and moss-covered trees and rocks.

European navigators explored some of the New Zealand fiords in the late eighteenth century. Captain Cook passed by Milford in 1770 and 1773 (probably because the entrance to the sound is hidden from the sea). He stopped farther south and rested his crew at a fiord he called Dusky Sound (so named because 'dusk' intervened before Cook could make harbor). It remained for a Welsh sealing captain named John Grono to discover Milford and name it after Milford Haven, near his place of birth.

Later Donald Sutherland, a Scot, became the first European settler in Milford Sound. He was known as the hermit of Milford; during his first two years there, he never saw another human.[9]

The Maoris had occupied Milford and other parts of Fiordland long ago, primarily on summer food-gathering expeditions. They also used Milford Sound as a source of greenstone (a type of jade) for ornament. The Maoris, who have lived in New Zealand for about a thousand years, have their own story as to how Fiordland was created.

The great sea god Tu-to-Rakiwhanoa was given the task of creating the fiords

EVENING TWILIGHT AT MILFORD SOUND.

out of solid mountain walls (in one version of the legend, the South Island was the petrified hull of a part-sunken canoe). Tu started from the south and used his axe to chop out the fiords. Owing to his inexperience, his initial efforts left 'ragged coastlines and many islands strewn about'. However, by the time he reached Milford, he had perfected his strokes, chopping 'cleanly and economical-ly', and creating the gem of a sound that exists today.[10]

According to a second legend, the wives of an early Polynesian explorer either ran away or were abducted to the west coast. The explorer chased them and found one of his wives in Milford Sound where she had been turned into greenstone. He wept and his tears penetrated the stone, marking it with flecks. The stone became known as *takiwai* or *tangiwai* (tears of weeping).[11]

Another Maori story is more recent. In the eighteenth century, there was bitter fighting among the southern Maori tribes. A group fled west to Te Anau (near the entrance to Fiordland National Park). Their pursuers caught them and killed part of the group, but some survived and retreated into the western forest. They took refuge in the remote retreats of Fiordland and became known as the 'Lost Tribe'. They are said to have remained there, living in peace and isolation until late in the nineteenth century.

Milford is the only sound in Fiordland that can be reached by road, and that access has only existed since 1954. In some months, many people come by coach or plane for a daytime cruise around the sound. Their visit tends to be brief, and there is only one hotel located at the sound. The road can be closed by storms at any time of year. Milford can also be reached by a hike of three or four days over the Milford Track, often termed 'the finest walk in the world'. The track was an ancient greenstone trail used by the Maoris.

Even when tour groups are present, Milford usually retains its peaceful atmosphere. It is also one of the few places for which the term awe-inspiring is truly appropriate. Its drawbacks are its wetness (an average of one hundred and sixty inches of rain each year with more than three hundred inches in a few years) and its sandflies (Captain Cook found them 'so troublesome they exceed everything of the kind I ever met with').

The view changes all the time. Fog often moves in at dawn, but, as it begins to lift, the snow-covered top of Mitre Peak can be glimpsed through openings in the fog and clouds. Soon sunlight grazes the peaks, which seem to glow like beacons.

As the day goes on, Mitre Peak seems to wear a number of masks and costumes like a character in a play and to display a variety of moods and expressions. Mitre Peak's moods are magnified, since the visitor sees the peak both directly and as reflected in the water. The still surface of the water seems a connection between the peaks and the visitor, and sometimes the visitor may find the mood of the place absorbed and reflected in his own feelings.

Milford Sound is most spectacular around sunset on a clear day. Though the setting sun cannot actually be seen, the glow in the sky sharply outlines Mitre Peak and its neighboring mountains, which are mirrored in the water. As I watched, a white heron circled and landed in the shallow water. Concentric circles radiated out, breaking up the reflection of Mitre Peak into jagged lines.

I found myself experiencing a variety of feelings simultaneously – exhilaration at the spectacular sights before me, great joy in the magnificence of nature, the comfort of being in a safe, protected place, and tearful gratitude for being so blessed as to have the opportunity to be in that wonderful place at a special time.

DIFFERENT MOODS OF MITRE PEAK.

BOWEN FALLS (ABOVE) IS ONLY ONE OF MANY
PLACES WHERE WATER CASCADES OVER ROCKS AND PLUNGES
INTO MILFORD SOUND.

KALALAU AND PU'UHONUA-O-HONAUNAU

Hawaii · USA

Hawaii has many tranquil sites, but two that I find unforgettable are the Kalalau Valley on the island of Kauai and Pu'uhonua-O-Honaunau on the island of Hawaii.

KALALAU VALLEY

Kauai is called the 'garden isle'; its north coast is wet, lush, and beautiful. The part of that coast called Na Pali (meaning 'the cliffs') has canyons with three thousand-foot walls. The cliffs have eroded into immense, sculpted landscapes, with some ridges having sharp-toothed edges and others looking like pleated fabrics. No roads penetrate the Na Pali coast, and access to its interior is primarily by a difficult eleven-mile hiking trail that usually takes two days to negotiate. At the heart of Na Pali is the Kalalau Valley, a remote, fertile valley with waterfalls and spectacular scenery.

Kalalau is sometimes called the 'Valley of Refuge'. Early Polynesians settled there, largely because the natural barriers of steep cliffs and rocky turbulent coast offered protection from neighboring tribes. For more than a thousand years, they lived in Kalalau peacefully and in isolation.

Kalalau was gradually abandoned in the nineteenth century, but in the 1950s it once again became a haven – this time for a medical doctor from the Virgin Islands, who experienced a religous conversion, gave away his possessions, and journeyed to Kalalau searching for truth. The doctor became known as the 'hermit of Kalalau' and remained there for many years. He found shelter in a cave and lived mainly off fruit and taro.

The doctor lived simply and found great pleasure in being close to nature. For him, 'of all the requirements for survival, beauty is the most important'.[12] In the Kalalau Valley, he felt 'very close to God'. As he said:

'My relationship to Him must be similar to that of Abraham's. There is more

THE KALALAU VALLEY ON KAUAI.

THE NA PALI COAST OF KAUAI

here than just quietness. There is a big peace. There is music in the wind and the surf.'[13]

The doctor became a legend, and in subsequent years others followed his example, hiking into Kalalau as part of their own search for truth.

PU'UHONUA-O-HONAUNAU

A *pu'uhonua* is a place of refuge or sacred sanctuary in Hawaii. The pu'uhonua at Honaunau is in the district of Kona on the west coast of the island of Hawaii.[14]

Until the early nineteenth century, a rigid system of laws, or *kapu*, governed the lives of the people of Hawaii. The kapu covered such subjects as the methods for worshiping the gods, the respect to be shown to royalty (for example, a

LATE AFTERNOON SUN AND CLOUDS, FROM THE KALALAU LOOKOUT.

commoner was required to prostrate himself in the presence of a chief), and the times for fishing and hunting. The kapu were sacred, and to break the kapu was to offend the gods and create the possibility that they might show their displeasure violently through an earthquake or other natural disaster. Breaking the kapu was often punishable by death.

If a person who violated the kapu managed to escape being killed on the spot, the only way he could assure his freedom was to reach a pu'uhonua, or a place of refuge, ahead of his pursuers. The pu'uhonua was sacred, and anyone reaching it was assured of safety. At the pu'uhonua, a ceremony of absolution or purification was performed. All was forgiven, and the kapu-breaker could return home as a free person. The pu'uhonua was also used in times of war – by women, children, and the elderly as a safe haven, and by warriors defeated in battle as the only place they could avoid being put to death by the victors.

There were many places of refuge in the Hawaiian islands. The one at Honaunau was historically the most important and is the best preserved. It is now a national park. Located on black lava rock and sand at the water's edge, it was separated from the palace grounds of the ruling chief by a massive wall formed from lava stones.

There was also a temple, or *heiau*, which gave the pu'uhonua its sanctity. The third temple built on the site has been recreated. It was originally constructed in 1650 in honor of Chief Keawe-i-keka-hi-alii-o-ka-moku. His bones were placed in the temple, and it was believed that the spiritual power (*mana*) in his bones provided additional protection to the pu'uhonua. In the next 168 years, the bones of twenty-two other chiefs were also placed there. The temple was guarded by carved images of gods, whose supernatural powers protected the temple and made it sacred. The images adjacent to the temple were related to Lono, who is associated with thunder, heavy rain, and lightning.

The platform that constituted the foundation of the second temple (built before 1550) can also be seen today. The first temple is marked only by a pile of black lava stones. On the other side of the wall, in the palace grounds, thatched buildings have been recreated, and techniques of mat weaving, fishing, and net making are demonstrated.

The visitor to Pu'uhonua-O-Honaunau can experience not only part of Hawaii's history but also the extraordinary tranquility of the site. The source of that tranquility may be the special combination of black lava rock, sand, palm trees, and ocean. It may also relate to the history of the place, the legends associated with it, or its sacred nature, all of which tend to make one treat the site with respect and reverence. Whatever the reason, the place has a special feeling that is perceptible. To get in touch with that feeling, one only needs to take the time to walk to the end of the park, sit on a rock in the shade of a palm tree at the edge of the water, and watch the gentle action of the waves.

The present-day visitor might also do well to pause and reflect for a moment on the people who occupied the place during earlier times – their wise use of limited natural resources, and their insistence on not taking more than they needed from the land or the sea.

SAND, BLACK LAVA, AND PALM TREES AT PU'UHONUA-O-HONAUNAU.

TEMPLE AT PU'UHONUA-O-HONAUNAU, PROTECTED
BY CARVED IMAGES OF GODS.

BIG SUR

California · USA

In 1771, the Spanish established Carmel Mission in what is now known as California. They called the wilderness to the south 'El Pais Grande del Sur' – the big country to the south. In the course of time, the phrase was shortened and became a combination of the English word 'big' and the Spanish word 'sur'. The rocky coast known as Big Sur extends for approximately seventy-five miles. Bounded on the west by the Pacific Ocean and on the east by the Santa Lucia Mountains, it is penetrated only by the Cabrillo Highway (Coast Highway 1).

Each turn in the highway reveals new beauty, and, even for the passing motorist, it is a memorable journey. For a person willing to invest more time, it can be a remarkable experience. Undistracted by golf courses, tennis courts, or other standard attractions of resort communities, and with television generally not available, the visitor to Big Sur tunes in to nature – to the sound of the sea, the smells of the eucalyptus and pine, and the sights of mountains plunging into the ocean, granite cliffs, and inaccessible beaches.

Along the Big Sur coastline are many wonderful places, including several state

ABOVE: THE COAST AT ESALEN.
LEFT: FOG MOVING TOWARD THE BIG SUR COAST NEAR LUCIA IN MORNING TWILIGHT.

parks and numerous hiking trails into wilderness areas. One of my favorites is Point Lobos at the northern end of Big Sur. Point Lobos, described by one artist as 'the greatest meeting of land and water in the world',[15] is a combination of headlands, irregular coves, and rolling meadows. A nature reserve for more than fifty years, its size was doubled in 1960 by the addition of a large underwater area that was the first underwater reserve in the United States.

The name Point Lobos is derived from the colonies of sea lions that can be seen on offshore rocks ('Punta de los Lobos Marinos', or Point of the Sea Wolves). In addition to two types of sea lions, other mammals frequently seen in the waters include sea otters, seals, and whales. The shore is a nesting and foraging site for large numbers of birds, and there are colorful displays of Indian paint brush, sea daisies, mock heather, poppies, buttercups, and lupine.

Point Lobos is best known as the site of the last original or primitive stand of the Monterey cypress, a tree that clings precariously to the cliffs and is bent into fascinating shapes by wind and weather. As has been said, 'the cypresses tell a poignant story of survival in a battle against great odds, twisting and buttressing themselves against the thrust of wind and pull of gravity, extracting vigor from the driving sea fogs and adapting themselves to drenching sprays of salt that sometimes crust the soil with white and rout the advance of other trees'.[16]

Before the arrival of the Europeans, Big Sur was occupied by Native Americans. The predominant tribe, the Esselens, lived south of Point Sur and used the thermal waters in Hot Springs Canyon. They often buried their dead on promontories that looked out to sea.

One of the areas used by the Esselens is now occupied by the Esalen Institute, founded in the early 1960s and sometimes referred to as a 'secular monastery' – a place 'where seekers of every description come to find light'.[17] Esalen provides workshops, seminars, and conferences that facilitate personal development, as well as a Soviet-American exchange program.

Esalen's classes offer intense learning experiences; its grounds offer tranquility and rejuvenation. Meditation in the garden in the early morning, with fog drifting in off the ocean, can be a mystical experience; equally so is watching in silence as the sun sets over the ocean on a clear evening, the view framed by the dark outlines of Monterey pines, or soaking in the thermal baths late at night, as the moon makes a trail of silver light across the water.

SUNSET FRAMED BY MONTEREY PINES AT ESALEN.

ABOVE: SURF AT POINT LOBOS.
RIGHT: LATE AFTERNOON VIEW FROM NEAR PARTINGTON POINT.

THE GANGES AT VARANASI

India

To Hindus, Varanasi is the most sacred place on earth. It is also one of the world's oldest cities, at least contemporary with Babylon and Thebes. Originally known as Kashi (or Kasha), meaning 'resplendent with divine light', it has also been known as Banaras (or Benares), the name adopted during Muslim rule.

The area is important to Buddhists as well as Hindus. It has been described as the birthplace of Buddhism, since it was at nearby Sarnath that Buddha first spoke to his disciples after achieving enlightenment. Yet Varanasi's primary spiritual significance, today as throughout much of its history, is to Hindus. Varanasi was Shiva's earthly abode, and the entire city is dedicated to Shiva. It has been called the navel of the world.

The importance of Varanasi is based on its location: on the banks of the sacred Ganges, the river of the great goddess, the connection to the Himalayas where the gods dwell. Every Hindu wants to make a pilgrimage to the Ganges at least once in his or her lifetime. Bathing in the Ganges offers purification, the chance to wash away all past sins. A bottle of water taken from the Ganges and brought back to the home is believed to have the power to cure future illnesses or assure the fertility of a new bride. Those fortunate enough to die near Varanasi and have their ashes spread upon the sacred waters may go directly to paradise and be released from the endless cycle of death and rebirth.

Every year, millions of pilgrims visit Varanasi, and every day at dawn there is a procession down to the river to bathe in the waters and offer prayers as the sun rises across the water. Even the non-Hindu feels like a pilgrim, wandering through the narrow streets as the city awakens. Suddenly, the visitor receives his first glimpse of the river. As he walks toward it the vista opens, and the full sweep of the river comes into sight – the broad, calm river, with sandbanks on the distant shore. Overhead, clouds take on hues of pink and gold.

Hindus walk down the terraced stone steps (the 'ghats') to the river's edge

BATHING IN THE PURIFYING WATERS OF THE GANGES.

and begin their ritual. Others arrange with a boatman to be rowed along the river so that they can watch the spectacle unfold. On one side, the first rays of sunlight paint broad golden brush strokes across the still water. On the other side, pilgrims bathe; holy men meditate and offer prayers; others wash their clothes, rinsing the garments in the river and beating them against flat rocks; and at the 'burning ghats', wood fires crackle, the flames devouring the bodies of fortunate Hindus.

The whole range of activities is riveting and almost overwhelming. Yet, for all the activity, there is also a calm and peace about the scene, giving it a unique grace. This quality stems partly from the broad expanse of the Ganges and its gentle flow and partly from the reverent attitude of pilgrims and holy men. Pilgrims stand waist-deep in the water, their eyes closed or raised to the heavens, their hands clasped in front of them, repeating the ancient *slokas* before fully immersing themselves in the purifying waters. Holy men (*saddhu*) sit on the steps or on platforms extending over the river, chanting or meditating.

Though many people are present, each is making his own individual journey, both external and internal. As has been said, the path of the Ganges is symbolic of man's journey: 'its unformed origins in hidden places far from human eyes; nourished into fullness; flowing through the broad and fertile plains where palaces and empires rose to dizzying heights, where people struggled desperately for power and pleasure; and in the end, all disappearing, merging with the sea'.[18] As the pilgrim approaches Mother Ganges, he reviews his own journey through life and comes face to face with his failures and highest aspirations. The scene is powerful, moving, and unforgettable.

SUNRISE OVER THE GANGES.

MEDITATION AND PRAYERS OFFERED BY PILGRIMS AND HOLY MEN
AT THE RIVER OF THE GREAT GODDESS.

Part Five

GARDENS

PRIVATE RETREATS

RHODODENDRONS AND AZALEAS AT LEONARDSLEE GARDENS, SUSSEX, ENGLAND.

Garden can be places for contemplation or meditation, and they can serve the same inspirational function as remote natural sites.

ZEN GARDENS: SETTINGS FOR MEDITATION

The Zen gardens of Japan emphasize simplification, purity of design and understatement. Pictured here are five Zen gardens in Kyoto.

ISLAMIC GARDENS: VISIONS OF PARADISE

The Islamic garden is a symbol of paradise, with shade and water as its archetypal elements. After summer heat and desert harshness, the Islamic garden provides a complete contrast, and its beauty is a reflection of God.

The Mughal gardens in Srinagar are a combination of Muslim philosophy and Hindu craftsmanship. In Muslim Spain, the Court of the Lions at the Alhambra brought the paradise garden into the living quarters, merging interior and exterior space. The setting of the Taj Mahal in India features a typical Islamic garden as well as a timeless view over river and farmland.

BRITISH WOODLAND GARDENS: DESCENDANTS OF THE SACRED GROVE

Sacred trees or sacred groves were common in many parts of the ancient world. Refuge could be found at the holy tree at Ephesus or at the sacred cypress grove at Phlius in Greece. Various Celtic and Germanic groups had sacred groves. Illustrated here is a wild, ancient grove of stunted oak trees in the moors of western England. The grove is thought to have been a last sanctuary of the Druids. It is contrasted with one of its descendants, the British woodland garden, in which the wildness of the sacred grove is tamed to create a more ordered arrangement of trees, shrubs, wild flowers, and pathways.

THE ZEN GARDENS
OF KYOTO

Japan

One garden in Kyoto consists entirely of two cones of pebbles resting on a bed of pebbles raked into curved lines. What kind of garden is this? Where are the flowers, the colors, the scents, the variety of textures? Without some introduction to Kyoto and to Zen Buddhism, the gardens of Kyoto – particularly the dry gardens – may well be a puzzle to the westerner.

In AD 794, the capital of Japan was moved from Nara to Kyoto, where it remained for more than a thousand years. Shintoism and Buddhism then existed side by side. Shintoism was native to Japan; Buddhism had come to Japan in the sixth century, originally through Korea and later directly from China. It quickly caught on and soon was declared the state religion. In the early years, Japanese Buddhism stayed close to the Chinese model. Japan's distinctive contribution to

SCORES OF VARIETIES OF MOSS CAN BE FOUND AT KOKEDERA
(SAIHOJI), THE 'MOSS TEMPLE' IN KYOTO.

A 'GREAT SEA' OF SAND, WITH TWO ISLANDS, AT THE DAISEN-IN TEMPLE, WITHIN DAITOKUJI.

Buddhism came hundreds of years later with the development of Zen Buddhism.

Zen is a shortened form of 'zenna', later 'zazen'. 'Za' in Chinese means to sit; 'Zen' comes from the Sanscrit term that means to contemplate. Literally, zazen is to contemplate in a sitting position. Zen Buddhism involves the practice of meditation and a simple, disciplined lifestyle, in the belief that through discipline and meditation a person can let go of all worldly desires and achieve enlightenment. By calming the mind, by quiet sitting, a person can dispel the illusions that tend to fill the mind and discover his or her true self. The best analogy is that of a jewel dropped into the water: '. . . to find the jewel, one must calm the waves . . . . Where the water of mediation is clear and calm, the mind-jewel will be naturally visible.'[1]

Zen Buddhism had its strongest effect on Japanese life in the period from the twelfth to the fifteenth century. Its influence was reflected in martial arts, the tea ceremony, flower arranging, and particularly landscape gardens. Nowhere is that influence more apparent than in Kyoto, which still has hundreds of Buddhist temples and monasteries, many with Zen gardens.

Zen gardens are designed for contemplation and meditation. Their elements are symbolic; in the example mentioned above, the cones of pebbles are generally thought to represent two island mountains that are points of stability in a sea of motion.[2] The scene is a representation of spiritual truths, an aid to understanding. Everything is simplified, and distractions are eliminated. The garden is both a philosophical statement and an object of aesthetic appreciation. In addition,

174

AN 'ISLAND' OF MOSS AND STONE IN THE ZEN ROCK GARDEN AT THE RYOANJI TEMPLE.

the meticulous grooming of the garden, such as the precise retracing of lines in the gravel, is a type of discipline that furthers spiritual development.

'Abstract compositions relying on understatement, simplicity, suggestion and implication were laid out, leaving room for the imagination but providing a starting point in the appreciation of everyday things . . . . The priest-gardeners were trying to present the truths and confusions and problems and joys that man encounters on his path to Zen enlightenment.'[3]

The garden may seem uninteresting at first, until you are drawn to take a closer look from the perspective of the wooden deck running round the perimeter of the temple. Here you sit, as others have done for hundreds of years, and look out at the garden.

Despite being in a modern city, the setting is quiet. As you gaze at the garden, you start to notice subtle details, such as the texture of the 'mountains'. Your focus shifts back and forth between the specific (the cones of pebbles) and the broader view (the sea with its tiny islands). Gradually, the curving 'waves' of pebbles seem to move and interact with the 'mountains'. Your mind embarks on a similar journey, and, in this contained, peaceful environment, thoughts about your own progress in life come to the surface.

Dry gardens can include large stones, mosses, bridges, paths, and even representations of waterfalls and streams. Other gardens are of *shakkei* style (borrowed scenery), where a view of a distant subject (such as a real mountain) is incorporated into the garden design.

A WATERFALL IN THE ZEN GARDEN
AT KINKAKUJI TEMPLE.

Some of the Zen gardens of Kyoto are immensely popular and are often filled with hundreds of uniformed Japanese schoolchildren. Ryoanji (created in 1500 by Soami), with its fifteen stones forming islands in a sea of raked pebbles, is the best-known example of a dry garden. It is not on the whole the ideal place for tranquility; indeed, its popularity has led to tape-recorded instructions about how to behave in the garden and even how long to meditate. Similarly, the Temple of the Golden Pavilion (Kinkakuji) and the Temple of the Silver Pavilion (Ginkakuji) rarely provide opportunities for solitude.

Yet there are so many Zen gardens in Kyoto that the visitor who seeks the authentic experience, and not the stereotype, will have no problem finding what he or she seeks.

I have two favorites. One is Shisendo, called the Poet's Temple because of portraits of ancient Chinese poets that line the walls of the study. Shisendo was a private retreat (or hermitage) built in 1641 by a scholar of Chinese classics and landscape architect who had also been an attendant to the Shogun. The garden of Shisendo is compact, offering many different views of several levels – some static, some in motion, some colorful, some providing overlapping textures, and some with the sound of running water. It is seldom crowded, and the small scale makes the experience very personal, very intimate.

My other favorite is Kokedera (Saihoji), the 'Moss Temple'. In order to visit this garden you have to make a reservation (and pay a large fee); the number of visitors is strictly limited.

On arrival, visitors are asked to take seats in the temple, where they are given a taste of the life of a Zen initiate. In front of them are inkwells, pens, and sheets of paper containing the characters needed for a Buddhist prayer. The instructors explain the prayer and chant it. Then, as a lesson in discipline, visitors are asked to trace the characters with their pens. After that, they are finally permitted to wander through the garden. Since visitors finish the writing exercise at different times, each individual (or family) ends up visiting the garden independently and making the tour at his or her own pace.

The garden, which was last redesigned about 650 years ago, is a sheer joy. A trail leads down to a pond with three islands and continues around the pond, past a tea-house and two small temples, and through a wooded area on a hillside. Every step provides a different view. The common element is moss – scores of

ABOVE AND LEFT: SHISENDO, THE 'POET'S TEMPLE'.

different varieties of moss covering every slope, every stone, and the bases of many trees. The scene is rich and lush. The color palette is limited, but, as with the dry gardens, that limitation seems only to enhance the intensity of the experience. Delicate maple trees add texture to the garden in the summer and color in the fall.

It is a beautiful scene; it can also seem somewhat sinister (especially on a rainy day) because of the twisted shapes of old branches, the murkiness of the water, and the darkness resulting from the dense foliage of taller trees. As I made the tour, I found myself pausing again and again and stepping as lightly as possible so as not to disturb the tranquility of the setting. It is impossible not to feel reverence for this special place. Sometimes I had to remind myself to take a deep breath and drink in the smells as well as the sights. Many visitors feel, on leaving Kokedera, that they do not wish to visit any other temple, for fear that it will seem an anticlimax. It probably will; Kokedera has few equals.

THE MUGHAL GARDENS
OF KASHMIR

India

Mughal Emperor Jahangir died on his last annual pilgrimage from the hot, dusty plains of India to the lush vale of Kashmir. His last words were 'Kashmir – only Kashmir'. Jahangir's son, Emperor Shah Jahan, the builder of the Taj Mahal, is reported to have said about Kashmir, and Srinagar in particular: 'If there is a paradise on earth, it is this . . . it is this . . . it is this.' The area around Srinagar in Kashmir is indeed lovely: a green valley with numerous lakes and springs, invigorating air, the Himalayas to the east and the Per Panjal range to the west, stately chinar trees and willows, flowering almonds, apples, apricots, cherries and peaches.

Srinagar would seem a strange place for Islamic gardens, which were developed in hot, dry, inhospitable places where the trees and flowing water of the garden provided relief from the unrelenting heat. There the garden contrasted with its setting, and, because of the contrast, the garden seemed a vision of paradise. In the case of Srinagar, where the setting already contains the elements of an earthly paradise, one could ask what need there is for an Islamic garden.

Yet the fact is that some of the most beautiful Islamic gardens that exist in the

ABOVE AND RIGHT: WATER GARDENS AT ACHABAL, SOUTHEAST OF SRINAGAR.

world today can be found in the area around Srinagar. The Mughal emperors loved the pleasant climate and peaceful setting of this idyllic spot, and their love is obvious from the elegant pleasure gardens arrayed around Dal Lake. The most famous of these gardens starts near the lake and extends up the hillside on a series of terraces. As a result, the view of the lake can be enjoyed from anywhere in the garden. A watercourse runs down the middle of the garden, directly towards the lake. Cascades, waterfalls, and fountains provide visual focal points and gentle sounds, as well as a sense of movement. Fruit trees and flower beds create delightful colorful displays and fill the air with sweet fragrances. Snow-covered mountains frame the view.

The most beautiful garden – and the best cared for – is Shalimar, built in about 1616 by Emperor Jahangir for his wife Nur Jahan, the 'light of the world'. Known today as the 'garden of love', it is on four terraces with a central water channel. At the center of the top terrace, which was reserved for the emperor and ladies of the court, is a dining pavilion with black marble pillars. The pavilion is surrounded by fountains, with waterfalls in front and behind.

The main problem with Shalimar is its popularity. It is often crowded, and there is even a 'son et lumière' show nightly during the season. An out-of-season visit is not the answer, as Srinagar can be cold and miserable in winter, and, in any case, the water is not turned on until mid-April (as I learned to my regret). The best solution, as with many of the places described in this book, is to go early in the day. Shalimar opens at sunrise, and the first few hours are the most enjoyable – a time when the only sounds are supplied by birds and flowing water.

Even better than Shalimar, for me anyway, is Achabal, a Mughal garden in a village about forty miles from Srinagar. The garden was probably started by Nur Jahan and was finished by the daughter of Shah Jahan in about 1640. The extensive watercourses are fed by a powerful spring at the top of the garden. There are three terraces, several cascades, numerous fountains in the main canal, and several pavilions. Because it is harder to reach, Achabal tends to be much less crowded and more peaceful than the gardens around Dal Lake. Ancient chinars provide shade as the visitor walks along the paths. Wild flowers push up through the grass, drawing the visitor for a closer look and tempting him to lie down and stretch out, look up at the trees, listen to the sounds of the fountains and the wind, and let the mind roam freely.

Achabal, seen from a pavilion surrounded by water.

AT SHALIMAR GARDENS, WATER FLOWS THROUGH A
CANAL, OVER CASCADES, AND AROUND A PAVILION USED BY EMPEROR
JEHANGIR AND THE LADIES OF THE COURT.

THE TAJ MAHAL AND ITS SETTING

India

Shah Jahan, Mughal 'Emperor of the World', was capable of cruelty and ruthlessness. He eliminated his brothers to assure his ascendancy to the throne, and, according to the legend, he ordered that the master craftsmen of the Taj Mahal should have their hands cut off so that they could never again create a structure as beautiful as the Taj.

He was also capable of great love. He was devoted to his grandfather, the Emperor Abkar, and especially to his wife, Mumtaz Mahal (the 'Jewel of the Palace'). When his beloved wife died following the birth of their fourteenth child, Shah Jahan went into a period of intense mourning. He was transformed into a white-haired old man whose back was bent. For the next twenty-two years, he lavished enormous amounts of money and energy on creating the Taj Mahal as a memorial to his wife – a monument designed to reflect the purity and beauty of their love.

THE TAJ MAHAL AND THE YAMUNA RIVER AT SUNRISE.

THE TAJ MAHAL SILHOUETTED BY EARLY MORNING LIGHT.

The Taj Mahal is probably the outstanding symbol of romantic love in all the world. It can be either inspiring or a large disappointment, depending on the mood of the visitor, his expectations, the crowds, and especially the time of day. The Taj is at its best in the stillness of dawn, when its symmetry, proportion, and elegance make a majestic impression.

In the context of this book, the Taj Mahal was selected not as an architectural triumph but as the focal point in a matchless setting. The mausoleum is first viewed from a massive gateway. The gateway 'symbolizes the transition from the realm of the senses to the realm of the spirit and is thus the entrance to paradise, the door to the womb of spiritual rebirth'.[4] Indeed, from the gateway, which frames the Taj Mahal and the watercourse leading up to it, the visitor feels on the threshold of another world, totally different from the world that exists on the other side of the wall. The contrast heightens the effect of that first view of the Taj, which can be breathtaking.

Between the gateway and the mausoleum is a walled Islamic garden that represents the perfection of Allah. The garden is divided by two intersecting watercourses into four equal parts (the number four signifying completeness). When the fountains are turned off and the air is still, the water channels are sheets of water that mirror the mausoleum. (The Muslim paradise is a mirror image, or opposite, of this world.)[5]

The other main feature of the Taj Mahal's setting is the river. From the marble plinth of the mausoleum, the views of the river and the undeveloped bank beyond (which is flooded during monsoon season) can be extraordinarily tranquil and soothing. In that landscape, it seems as if time has stood still for centuries.

During the early morning, when a heavy mist often hangs over the river, you may witness an incomparable scene. On the other side of the river, one can make out a red tower near the site where Shah Jahan intended to build his own mausoleum. A man with two camels walks slowly toward the river. Raising his clothing above his knees, he starts across, the camels following behind. The river is shallow; the man and his camels wade off into the mist. Several minutes later, they reach the other side and continue on through the fields.

The mist disperses. A woman with an earthen pot on her head walks to the river, fills the pot, places it on her head, walks a few yards to a vegetable garden, empties the pot, places it on her head, and returns to the river – again and again and again. Two eagles walk along the river bank. The unfolding scene is captivating, and the visitor is drawn to sit on a bench, empty his mind, and simply observe.

In the space of a few minutes, the visitor sees three different worlds: the noisy, crowded and impoverished city of Agra; the beautiful oasis that is the walled garden; and the timeless view of river and fields. In the middle of it all is the Taj Mahal, the symbolic masterpiece that brings these worlds together.

THE TIMELESS VIEW OVER
THE RIVER FROM THE TERRACE OF
THE TAJ MAHAL.

THE GARDEN COURTS OF THE ALHAMBRA

Spain

After Córdoba was recaptured by the Christians in the thirteenth century, Granada became the principal Muslim stronghold in Spain. Under the Nasrid dynasty, Muslim architecture reached its peak in the fourteenth century at the Palace of the Alhambra (Alcazar). The Alhambra is an unsurpassed example of decoration for its own sake – decoration in stucco, tile and wood, covering walls and ceilings.

At the heart of the palace is the Court of the Lions. In the middle is a massive fountain, pavilions are at each end, and important chambers open off the court, all connected by arcades. The court has grace, lightness, and perfection of scale.

The relevance of the Alhambra to this book is the way its designers used garden courts (and particularly the Court of the Lions) to bring the Islamic garden right into the living quarters. There is a total integration of interior and exterior space. Paradise is brought indoors.

At the Court of the Lions, a water channel starting in one living space leads the eye out of that room through multiple arches, across the court, past the fountain, through more arches on the other side of the court, and into another

ABOVE: THE CENTRAL FOUNTAIN, COURT OF THE LIONS.
LEFT: THE INTERIOR OF A PAVILION IN THE COURT OF THE LIONS AT THE ALHAMBRA.

ABOVE: THE COURT OF THE CANAL AT THE GENERALIFE.
RIGHT: THE COURT OF THE LIONS.

living space. Slender columns frame the view. From behind the pavilions that extend into the court, the vista is even more complex; a water channel leads the eye into and through a pavilion (in effect a 'room' with rows of columns in place of walls) and across the courtyard to a mirror image of the same arrangement on the other side. In earlier times, flowers would have softened the view and added color and scent. The courtyard imposes order on the adjacent enclosed spaces and modulates the transition between them. The pavilions and colonnades act as intermediaries between gardens and enclosed rooms.

Nearby is the Generalife, a place of relaxation for the Moorish kings of Granada with many gardens on different levels. Again, the most impressive aspect is the use of the court, especially the Court of the Canal, which is integrated with interior spaces at both ends by the use of open arches supported on columns. Water cascades into the long pool from multiple fountain-jets hidden in the foliage. From the end of the court, the visitor, soothed by the gentle sound of falling water, looks inward to the intimate garden or outward to the Alhambra and the city below.

ABOVE: ARCHES LEADING TO THE COURT OF THE LIONS.
RIGHT: DARAXA BELVEDERE FROM THE HALL OF THE TWO SISTERS, COURT OF THE LIONS.

BRITISH WOODLAND GARDENS

Descendants of the Sacred Grove

Wistman's Wood is located on the moors of Devonshire in southwest England. It is a wild and remote part of Dartmoor on a hillside along the West Dart River. The wood is believed to have been a principal sanctuary of the Druids, their sacred grove, a place where rites and ceremonies were performed, and it may have been one of their last places of refuge in the west of England.[6] Above it, on top of the hill, is a huge pile of stones said to be the burial chamber of a Druidic chieftain.

Wistman's Wood is a strange place – stunted oak trees among a clutter of granite boulders. Many of the trees are hundreds of years old but only ten to fifteen feet high. Branches and roots are twisted into strange, disquieting shapes, shapes reminiscent of the poisonous snakes that are supposed to live in the grove.

GRANITE BOULDERS (ABOVE) AND A STUNTED OAK TREE (LEFT) AT WISTMAN'S WOOD ON DARTMOOR.

Moss climbs the tree trunks and drips from the twisted branches. The stones are covered with lichens and mosses, with ferns growing between them. Some of the upright stones look like megaliths; other flat ones look like grave markers.

The wood has an eerie atmosphere even in summer sunlight. The dense leaves filter out most of the light; what little there is dapples the rocks and makes the moss glow a rusty green. On a dark day in winter, when the trees are bare and the branches look even more like the snakes on Medusa's head or when a cold wind is howling across the moor, the wood can be terrifying.

According to local legend, Wistman's Wood is haunted. It is the place from which the Devil emerges at midnight, riding a headless black horse and accompanied by ferocious black dogs with red eyes. Anyone unfortunate enough to see them, it is said, will die within a year.[7]

It is easy to understand why the wood is reputed to be haunted. At the same time, it is a captivating, very beautiful setting. It is a wild place where, as in life, both peaceful and sinister qualities coexist. Which one predominates at any given time depends on the weather and the mood of the viewer.

In contrast, the British woodland garden tames the wildness and removes the sinister qualities. Pheasants take the place of spirit creatures; wild flowers, azaleas and rhododendrons replace twisted roots and gnarled branches. Exotic trees and shrubs are arrayed along winding paths. The effect is a romantic or picturesque version of nature – a place for walking and contemplation, a place for conversation, a place for unalloyed admiration of natural beauty.

Whether the woodland is wild or tamed, the British have always appreciated the benefits of solitude among the trees. As Edmund Waller wrote in the seventeenth century:

> Near this my Muse what most delights her, sees
> A living gallery of aged trees . . .
> In such green palaces the first kings reigned,
> Slept in their shades, and angels entertained;
> With such old counsellors they did advise,
> And, by frequenting sacred groves, grew wise.
> Free from the impediments of light and noise,
> Man, thus retired, his nobler thoughts employs.[8]

THE WILDNESS OF WISTMAN'S WOOD (TOP),
CONTRASTED WITH A MORE CIVILIZED WALK AT EXBURY GARDENS (BOTTOM).

PATHS ALONG THE
RIVER HIRAETHLYN AT
THE WOODLAND DELL AT
BODNANT, WALES.

THE CASCADE AT
BOWOOD, WILTSHIRE,
CREATED IN THE 1780s
BY CHARLES HAMILTON.

THE WOODLAND GARDEN AT
LEONARDSLEE, SUSSEX.

EPILOGUE

BORA BORA, FRENCH POLYNESIA.

The process of creating this book has been an extraordinary experience. Among other things, it involved seemingly endless travel to thirteen countries on five continents and countless hours in airports waiting for planes. It involved more than a hundred nights by myself in anonymous hotels, where the usual routine seemed to consist primarily of eating mediocre meals, washing out socks and underwear, and bumping into walls in the middle of the night while trying to find the bathroom.

Hauling around cameras, lenses, tripod, other photographic equipment, clothes, and research materials made me feel like a beast of burden much of the time, and constant packing and unpacking seemed to occupy most of the rest. I had anxious moments trying to get hundreds of rolls of film through airport security and customs inspections, including more than one occasion when every box of film was opened and every roll of film was taken out of its canister and examined.

I spent many long days watching hopefully for the rain to stop or the grey skies to clear. I experienced frustrating delays waiting to photograph a site without people in the picture, only to find that Pipkin's Law was in effect (that is, when one group of visitors finally finishes what it is doing and slowly moves away, another group inevitably moves into the picture). At one location, I waited more than two hours to photograph a scene without people, and, by the time I finally had a clear shot, the sun was gone.

However, the inconveniences were relatively minor and the joys *far* outweighed the tribulations. The vast majority of the places featured in this book were new to me and were places I had always wanted to see. The book provided both the opportunity and the motivation to visit them, and it gave me a special reason to maximize the intensity of the experience at each site.

The book allowed me to learn a considerable amount about subjects I found fascinating, especially information about earlier peoples and the relevance of their beliefs to our lives today. It also gave me the chance to sample a wide variety of natural settings and draw my own conclusions about the kinds of places I find most satisfying.

It enabled me to make some progress in my personal search for tranquility. In addition, it facilitated examination of my own belief structure and observation of my thoughts, feelings, and behavior in a way that does not happen when I am in my usual surroundings.

It also allowed me to see the similarities and interrelationships of people all over the planet, demonstrating once again that we all have the same fundamental goals and we are all in it together. It reaffirmed that warmth and generosity are universal human traits and that those characteristics seem to be manifested most abundantly in small towns and rural areas. I will never forget the kindness shown to me by people to whom I was a total stranger – people who extended assistance without any thought of reward or reciprocation for their generous actions. Several of these experiences occurred in Turkey, including one occasion when a man at a gas station drove fourteen miles out of his way to make sure that I reached my destination and then smiled and disappeared.

Most of all, the book provided many joyous moments – moments in unimaginably beautiful places, when all conditions were perfect and when I felt uniquely privileged to have the opportunity to be there at that time. Milford Sound and Ayers Rock at sunset, the Taj Mahal and the Matterhorn at dawn, Monument Valley and Cappadocia in the snow, Carnac and Big Sur in the fog, the Moss Temple in gentle rain – all were incredible experiences for which I am truly grateful.

For anyone interested in the technical side of the photographs, there is not a lot to say, since I tried to make the photography as simple as possible. To lighten the load, I used only 35mm equipment (specifically two Nikon F3 camera bodies and six Nikon lenses). I shot only slide film (mainly Kodachrome 25 and 64, with some Fujichrome 50) and used a tripod most of the time. Two of the photographs were taken with a split-screen filter to darken the sky. Other than that, I avoided using any filters; the natural colors were so wonderful that I wanted to let them come through without manipulation or artificial enhancement.

I cannot conclude without expressing my gratitude to seven special friends. Jeanne Cameron deserves much of the credit for the fact that the focus of the book shifted from religious retreats to special places in nature. Jeanne also encouraged the inclusion of prehistoric sites, and her resonance to certain abstract or symbolic images had a significant effect on my own vision. Colin Webb suggested the book, made it possible financially, and stayed with me as my thinking evolved. Gill Ravenel and Frances Smyth gave me the benefit of their discerning eyes and provided continuing enthusiatic support that was invaluable, especially when my own confidence flagged. Jim McHugh, Margaret Nea, and Marguerite Millhauser reviewed drafts and encouraged me to let the real James Pipkin (whoever that may be) come through in the book.

My thanks to all of them and also: to my law partners at Steptoe & Johnson, who tolerated the absences that were necessary for me to do this book; to the Departmental Office of Tourism of the Dordogne, which supplied the photographs of Lascaux II (see page 59); to Malcolm Voci, who helped with the manuscript; to my mother, whose enjoyment of travel rubbed off on me; and to the guiding spirit who watches over me and provides opportunities such as this that enrich and enhance my life.

DAWN OVER THE ATLANTIC, FROM ACADIA NATIONAL PARK, MAINE.
OVERLEAF: DAWN AT MONUMENT VALLEY.

NOTES

Introduction

1 See, e.g., John Michell, *The Traveler's Key to Sacred England*, pp. 237-8.
2 The Venerable Bede, *Vita S. Cuthberti*, quoted by Helen Waddell in *The Desert Fathers*, pp. 15-16.
3 Sir Richard Burton, *Personal Narrative of a Pilgrimage to Al-Madinah and Mecca*, quoted by John Julius Norwich in *A Taste For Travel*, pp. 398-9.
4 Quotations are from C.G. Jung, *Memories, Dreams, Reflections* (Aniela Jaffe, ed.), pp. 77-8.
5 Quoted in Ian Cameron, *Lost Paradise*, p. 13.
6 Id., p. 10.

Part One Deserts: Places of Purification

1 *Larousse World Mythology*, p. 1597.
2 Estimates vary; grinding stones found in the area date from approximately twenty thousand years ago, though it is believed that the area was occupied for thousands of years prior to that.
3 This story and others appear in Robert Layton's book, *Uluru, an Aboriginal History of Ayers Rock*, pp. 5-16. See also Charles P. Mountford, *Aboriginal Conception Beliefs*, pp. 29-34.
4 A. W. Reed, *Aboriginal Stories of Australia*, p. 8.
5 Id., p. 7.
6 Robert Layton, supra, p. 15.
7 Bruce Chatwin, *The Songlines*, p. 13.
8 Id., p. 14.
9 Robert Layton, supra, p. 12.
10 Ibid.
11 See Otto F.A. Meinardus, *Monks and Monasteries of the Egyptian Deserts*, pp. 33-5.
12 Id., pp. 1-4.
13 Helen Waddell, *The Desert Fathers*, pp. 1-5.
14 Evangelos Papaioannou, *The Monastery of St. Catherine*, p. 6.
15 Id., p. 13.

Part Two Caves: Places of rebirth

1 Pierre Fanlac (ed.), *Lascaux en Périgord Noir*, p. 42.
2 Because of conservation concerns, access to Lascaux is now strictly limited. Most visitors see a meticulously created replica, Lascaux II, which has the exact dimensions of the original and was painted with natural colors and ancient techniques.
3 Joseph Campbell, *Historical Atlas of World Mythology*, vol. 1, pt 1, p. 60.

4 Dates are estimated by Dr. T. V. Pathy in *Ajanta, Ellora and Aurangabad Caves: An Appreciation*.
5 See John Snelling, *The Sacred Mountain*, p. 16.
6 Alistair Shearer, *The Traveler's Key to Northern India, A Guide to the Sacred Places of Northern India*, p. 59.
7 Ibid.
8 Frank Waters, *The Book of the Hopi*, p. 129.
9 Id., p. 24.
10 Richard Amber, *The Anasazi, Prehistoric People of the Four Corners Region*, p. 46.
11 Frank Waters, supra, p. 129.

Part Three Mountains: Abode of the Gods

1 See, e.g., Dolores LaChapelle, *Earth Wisdom*, pp. 15-19.
2 *Larousse World Mythology*, supra, p. 1602.
3 Ibid.
4 John Snelling, *The Sacred Mountain*, pp. 217-18.
5 Id., p. 41.
6 Dolores LaChapelle, *Earth Wisdom*, p. 51.
7 John Snelling, *supra*, p. 197.
8 Lama Anagarika Govinda, *The Way of the White Clouds*, p. 197.
9 Id., p. 198.
10 Id., pp. 207-8.
11 Elizabeth V. Reyes, *Bali*, p. 38.
12 Michael Covarrubias, *The Island of Bali*.
13 Willard A. Hanna, *Bali Profile*.
14 Silvio Santosa, *Bali, What and Where*, p. 86.
15 Elizabeth V. Reyes, supra, p. 19.
16 Ibid.
17 Peter Boardman, *Sacred Summits*, p. 14.
18 Ibid.
19 Phillippe Joutard, *L'Invention du Mont Blanc*, p. 19.
20 Maurice Gay and Marie-Francis Balmet, *Les Maudites Glaciers, Les Pellarins*.
21 The name may be traced to Martha Longmire's first visit in 1885, when she exclaimed, 'It looks just like Paradise.'
22 Pat O'Hara and Tim McNulty, *Mount Rainier National Park, Realm of the Sleeping Giant*, p. 22.
23 Ella E. Clark, *Indian Legends of the Pacific Northwest*, pp. 7-8.
24 Id., pp. 31-2. See also Arthur D. Martinson, *Wilderness Above the Sound*, p. 6.

Part Four Seacoasts: Return to Source

1 *Larousse World Mythology*, supra, p. 3002.
2 The term 'megalith' comes from the Greek word 'megas', meaning 'large', and 'lithos', meaning 'stone'.
3 See, e.g., Gerald Hawkins, *Stonehenge Decoded*.
4 See, e.g., Charles Le Quintrec, *The Stones of Carnac*, p. 4.
5 Information in this paragraph is taken primarily from John Green, *Carnac and the Megalithic Monuments of the Morbihan*, pp. 22-4.
6 Gerald and Margaret Ponting, *New Light on the Stones of Callanish*, p. 32.
7 See, e.g., Hellmuth and Beatrice Schulz, *Callanish*, p. 16.
8 See, e.g., id., pp. 28-31, and *New Light on the Stones of Callanish*, supra, pp. 44-52.
9 John Cobb, *Fiordland . . . the incredible wilderness*, p. 82.
10 *Mountains of Water, the Story of Fiordland National Park*, Department of Lands Survey, Fiordland National Park, p. 82. See also *Fiordland . . . the incredible wilderness*, supra, p. 82.
11 Diana and Jeremy Pope, *South Island*, p. 244.
12 Quoted in *Kauai*, Bob Krauss and Bill Gleasner, p. 56 (6th ed. 1987).
13 Ibid.
14 See, e.g., *Pu'uhonua-O-Honaunau*, National Park Service; and *Pu'uhonua-O-Honaunau: Place of Refuge*, Jerry Y. Shimoda, the Environment Journal, National Parks & Conservation Magazine (Feb. 1975), p. 4.
15 See *Point Lobos; Interpretation of a Primitive Landscape* (Joseph H. Engbeck, Jr., ed.), p. 13, quoting the landscape painter Francis McComas.
16 Id., p. 17 (Frederick Law Olmsted Jr and George B. Vaughan).
17 Rick Tarnas, description of Esalen dated Fall 1978.
18 Steven Darian, *A Ganges of the Mind: Journey on the River of Dreams*.

Part Five Gardens: Private Retreats

1 *How to Practise Zazen*, Institute for Zen Studies, Kyoto, p. 21.
2 Islands are also 'representative of the isles of the Blest, where the immortal souls live'. A. K. Davidson, *The Art of Zen Gardens*, p. 36.
3 Id., p. 23.
4 Alistair Shearer, *The Traveler's Key To Northern India, A Guide to the Sacred Places of Northern India*, p. 282.
5 Id., p. 287.
6 John Michell, *The Traveler's Key to Sacred England*, p. 170.
7 See, e.g., John Pegg, *After Dark on Dartmoor: Collected Legends and Tales*, p. 12.
8 'Ode on St. James Park', *The Poems of Edmund Waller* (G. Thorn Drury, ed.) (1893), p. 170, quoted by Miles Jebb in the *Thames Valley Heritage Walk*.

BIBLIOGRAPHY

Amber, Richard, *The Anasazi, Prehistoric People of the Four Corners Region*, Museum of Northern Arizona, Flagstaff, 1977.

Burton, Sir Richard, *Personal Narrative of a Pilgrimage to Al-Madinah and Mecca*, Longman & Co., London, 1855-6.
Boardman, Peter, *Sacred Summits*, Arena, London, 1982.
Brookes, John, *Gardens of Paradise*, New Amsterdam Books, New York, 1987.

Cameron, Ian, *Lost Paradise*, Salem House Publishers, Topsfield, Massachusetts, 1987.
Campbell, Joseph, *Historical Atlas of World Mythology*, Harper & Row, New York, 1988.
Campbell, Joseph, *The Power of Myth*, Doubleday, New York, 1988.
Chatwin, Bruce, *The Songlines*, Jonathan Cape, London, 1987.
Clark, Ella E., *Indian Legends of the Pacific Northwest*, University of California Press, Berkeley, California, 1953.
Cobb, John, *Fiordland . . . the incredible wilderness*, Cobb/Horwood Publications, Auckland, New Zealand, 1987.

Darian, Steven, *A Ganges of the Mind: Journey on the River of Dreams*, Ratna Sagar, Delhi, 1988.
Davidson, A.K., *The Art of Zen Gardens*, Jeremy P. Tarcher, Los Angeles, California, 1983.

Engbeck, Joseph H., Jr (ed.), *Point Lobos, Interpretation of a Primitive Landscape*, State of California Department of Parks and Recreation, 1963.

Fanlac, Pierre, (ed.), *Lascaux en Périgord Noir*, Pierre Fanlac, Périgueux, 1982.

Gay, Maurice, and Balmet, Marie-Francis, *Les Maudites Glaciers, Les Pellarins*, Comite d'Organisation du Bicentenaire, Chamonix, 1986.
Govinda, Lama Anagarika, *The Way of the White Clouds*, Shambhala, Boston, 1988.

Hawkins, Gerald, S., *Stonehenge Decoded*, Hippocrene Books, New York, 1988.
How to practice Zazen, Institute for Zen Studies, Kyoto.

Jacoby, Mario, *Longing for Paradise*, Sigo Press, Boston, 1985.
Jebb, Miles, *Thames Valley Heritage Walk*, Constable, London, 1980.
Joutard, Philippe, *L'Invention du mont Blanc*, Collection Archives, Gallimard/Julliard, Saint-Amand, France, 1986.

Julyan, Robert Hixson, *Mountain Names,* The Mountaineers, Seattle, Washington, 1984.

Jung, C.G., *Memories, Dreams, Reflections,* (Aniela Jaffe, ed.), Vintage Books, New York, 1965.

Krauss, Bob, and Gleasner, Bill, *Kauai,* Island Heritage, Honolulu, Hawaii, 6th ed., 1987.

LaChapelle, Dolores, *Earth Wisdom,* Finn Hill Arts, Silverton, Colorado, 1978.

Larousse World Mythology, Excalibur Books, New York, 1984.

Layton, Robert, *Uluru, an Aboriginal History of Ayers Rock,* Australian Institute of Aboriginal Studies, Canberra, 1986.

Le Quintrec, Charles, *The Stones of Carnac,* Ouest France, Rennes, 1980.

Martinson, Arthur D., *Wilderness Above the Sound,* Northland Press, Flagstaff, Arizona, 1986.

Meinardus, Otto F.A., *Monks and Monasteries of the Egyptian Deserts,* The American University in Cairo Press, Cairo, 1989.

Michell, John, *Megalithomania,* Cornell University Press, Ithaca, New York, 1982.

Michell, John, *The Traveler's Key to Sacred England,* Alfred A. Knopf, New York, 1988.

Mountains of Water, the Story of Fiordland National Park, Department of Lands Survey, Fiordland National Park, Cobb/Horwood Publications, Auckland, New Zealand, 1986.

Mountford, Charles P., *Aboriginal Conception Beliefs,* Hyland House, Melbourne, 1981.

Munro, Eleanor, *On Glory Roads,* Thames and Hudson, New York, 1987.

Norwich, John Julius, *A Taste for Travel,* Alfred A. Knopf, New York, 1987.

O'Hara, Pat, and McNulty, Tim, *Mount Rainier National Park, Realm of the Sleeping Giant,* Woodlands Press, Del Mar, California, 1985.

Papaioannau, Evangelos, *The Monastery of St. Catherine,* Isis Press, Cairo, 1980.

Pathy, Dr T.V., *Ajanta, Ellora and Aurangabad Caves: An Appreciation,* Pathy Aurangabad, 1987.

Pegg, John, *After Dark on Dartmoor: Collected Legends and Tales,* John Pegg Pub., Tunbridge Wells, 1984.

Ponting, Gerald and Margaret, *New Light on the Stones of Callanish,* Essprint Ltd, Stornoway, Scotland, 1984.

Pope, Diana and Jeremy, *South Island,* Mobil New Zealand Travel Guide, Reed Methuen, Auckland, 1986.

Pu'uhonua-O-Honaunau, National Park Service, U.S. Department of the Interior, Washington, D.C., 1988.

Reed, A.W., *Aboriginal Stories of Australia,* Reed Books, Frenchs Forest, New South Wales, 1980.

Reyes, Elizabeth V., *Bali,* Times Editions, Singapore, 1987.

Santosa, Silvio, *Bali, What and Where,* Guna Agung, Bali, 1981.

Schulz, Hellmuth and Beatrice, *Callanish,* B.M. Schulz, Callanish, Scotland, 1986.

Shearer, Alistair, *The Traveler's Key to Northern India, a Guide to the Sacred Places of Northern India,* Knopf, New York, 1985.

Shimoda, Jerry Y., *Pu'uhonua-O-Honaunau: Place of Refuge,* The Environmental Journal, National Parks & Conservation Magazine, February 1975.

Snelling, John, *The Sacred Mountain,* East West Publications, London, 1983.

Storr, Anthony, *Solitude, A Return to the Self,* The Free Press, New York, 1988.

Waddell, Helen, *The Desert Fathers,* Ann Arbor Paperbacks, The University of Michigan Press, Michigan, 1957.

Waters, Frank, *The Book of the Hopi,* Penguin Books, New York, 1987.